Barack Obama

Barack Obama

THE VOICE OF AN AMERICAN LEADER

Joann F. Price

GREENWOOD PRESS

Westport, Connecticut ● London

Library of Congress Cataloging-in-Publication Data

Price, Joann F.
   Barack Obama : the voice of an American leader / Joann F. Price.
     p. cm.
   Includes bibliographical references and index.
   ISBN 978-0-313-36236-1 (alk. paper)
   1. Obama, Barack—Quotations. 2. Obama, Barack—Political and social views.
3. Legislators—United States—Quotations. 4. Legislators—Illinois—Quotations.
5. Presidential candidates—United States—Quotations. 6. Presidents—United States—
Election—2008—Quotations, maxims, etc. 7. United States—Politics and government—
2001—Quotations, maxims, etc. 8. Illinois—Politics and government—1951—
Quotations, maxims, etc. 9. United States—Social conditions—1980—Quotations,
maxims, etc. 10. Racially mixed people—United States—Quotations. I. Title.
E901.1.O23P755 2009
328.73092—dc22   2008035007

British Library Cataloguing in Publication Data is available.

Library of Congress Catalog Card Number: 2008035007
ISBN: 978-0-313-36236-1

First published in 2009

Greenwood Press, 88 Post Road West, Westport, CT 06881
An imprint of Greenwood Publishing Group, Inc.
www.greenwood.com

Printed in the United States of America

∞

The paper used in this book complies with the
Permanent Paper Standard issued by the National
Information Standards Organization (Z39.48-1984).

10 9 8 7 6 5 4 3 2 1

To Bob, always
and to Holly, love from the first moment

Contents

Introduction

"In no other country on earth is my story even possible."[1]

By any measure, the 2008 presidential race has been historic, but it has also created an enthusiasm and a higher degree of interest in politics few have seen before. For a sense of what has transpired in this race and the reasons for, at least in part, how this race is different from others in America's history, this book looks at one candidate, Barack Obama, from the perspective of quotations presented in thematic chapters on topics ranging from heritage and family to state and national politics and race and religion. These quotations by and about Obama, the first African American to be his party's presidential nominee, provides a look at the candidate who would face Republican John McCain, the senator from Arizona, in the general election.

The primary season for the 2008 campaign for the presidency began earlier than any other election in history and would take nearly two years to play out. As a crowded field of candidates on both sides of the political aisle announced their intention to run for their party's nomination, many braced themselves for a long, arduous campaign. However, as the season got underway and progressed, many in America were surprised by what was taking shape. While there were many of the usual candidates in the race, this time there were two new politicians making a bid for the highest office in the land. For the first time in history, a woman and a black man were in the race; both were viable candidates and both had clear shots at winning the nomination. In a short while, they were the Democratic Party's frontrunners. Senator Hillary Clinton and Senator Barack Obama each made the race historic, and for many voters, very compelling. People all across the country were enthusiastic, and the world noticed. All across America, people were talking and listening and getting involved.

As the primary season got underway, with the first caucus in Iowa and the first primary in New Hampshire held in early January 2008, the candidates took their message from state to state. Throughout the primary season, people stood for hours in searing heat, blowing snow, drenching rain, and frigid cold and waited in venues so crowded that the overflow had to stand outside. It wasn't enough just to attend caucuses and vote in primaries; it was also important to speak up and get involved. In rural communities and urban areas, in crowded neighborhoods and inner cities, on farmlands and on sidewalks, people were getting involved in huge numbers not seen before.

The enthusiasm in the election for the presidency was no doubt created in part by a phenomenon known as Barack Obama. Because of this tall, lanky freshman senator from Illinois, something changed in American politics. There was an energy few had seen or felt before, and it meant that perhaps there might be a new vision of America around the world. As the primary and caucus calendar progressed, candidates in both parties dropped out of the race, and for the Democrats, the campaign became a contest between Barack Obama and Hillary Clinton. And while John McCain became the presumptive nominee for the Republican Party fairly early in the process, the Obama and Clinton campaigns continued primary after primary, caucus after caucus. Supporters for both candidates fought on too. They campaigned, donated, and attended rallies. People registered in record numbers to vote and participated in their state's primary or caucus. Both candidates stumbled, both candidates tried to stick to the issues, and both candidates wanted desperately to win. There was talk about a "dream ticket" where one would be president and the other vice president, and while many voters and pundits liked this idea, no one knew who would be at the top of the ticket and who would be the running mate. Neither candidate wanted to address this possibility; both were sure they were the best candidate to be president.

It was Representative John Lewis, a civil rights icon and one of America's most influential black congressmen, who said of Obama: "Something's happening in America, something some of us did not see coming. Barack Obama has tapped into something that is extraordinary."[2] It is because of this "something extraordinary" that a look at the candidate that some describe as the most charismatic politician to come along in a very long time is appropriate. It is because the campaign coincides with a time that most recognize as one of the most crucial and difficult in our nation's history. Indeed, the next president will have the job of directing the country through many difficult issues (including two wars, a strained, tumultuous economy, and a planet in peril) and restoring America's stature in the world. Thus, getting to know Obama through what he has to say about his life and the issues of the day and what others have to say about him and the issues is compelling. The quotations, with introductions that preface each chapter, cover Obama's heritage, family, years in state and national office, his run for the presidency, the issues of the day, community activism and service, and race, country, and citizenship. There are certainly many more quotations that could have been included; however, this is meant to be a sample of what has been said by and about the man that has helped create a grassroots movement in American politics and has caused a stir in this country and around the world.

At the Commencement Address at Knox College in Galesburg, Illinois on June 4, 2005, Obama said, "The true test of the American ideal is whether we're able to recognize our failings and then rise together to meet the challenges of our time. Whether we allow ourselves to be shaped by events and history, or whether we act to shape them."[3]

NOTES

1. Barack Obama, Democratic National Convention, July 27, 2004.
2. Tim Reid and Tom Baldwin, "Hillary Clinton suffers new blow as civil rights icon says he's seen the light," *TimesOnline*, February 28, 2008, http://www.timesonline.co.uk (accessed February 28, 2008).
3. Barack Obama, "Commencement Address, Knox College, June 4, 2005," http://www.americanrhetoric.com (accessed June 11, 2008).

CHAPTER 1

On Heritage, Marriage, and Children

"What's interesting is how deeply American I feel, considering this exotic background. Some of it is the Midwestern roots of my grandparents, my mother, and the values that they reflect. But some of it is also a deep abiding sense that what is quintessentially American, is all these different threads coming together to make a single quilt. And I feel very much like I'm one of those threads that belong in this quilt, that I'm a product of all these different forces, black, white, Asian, Hispanic, Native American. That, somehow, all this amalgam is part of who I am, and that's part of the reason I love this country so much."[1]

"My experience growing up in Indonesia or having family in small villages in Africa—I think makes me much more mindful of the importance of issues like personal security or freedom from corruption. I've witnessed it in much more direct ways than I think the average American has witnessed it."[2]

Introduction

Until Barack Obama made his historic speech at the Democratic National Convention on July 27, 2004, few knew him. He began the speech by saying, "Tonight is a particular honor for me because, let's face it, my presence on this stage is pretty unlikely." In the speech, Barack introduced himself to the country and to the world. The son of a white woman from Kansas and a black man from Kenya, Barack told his unique story, a story of growing up in Hawaii and Indonesia; about being raised by his mother and her parents, Madelyn (Toots) and Stanley Dunham, after his father returned to Africa when he was just 2 years old. Barack told the stories of his father's large African family that he came to know as an adult. In his electrifying speech that night, and in speeches, interviews, and town hall meetings ever since, Obama has introduced himself to the nation and the world as he talks about his dreams and his abiding faith in the possibilities of the United States of America. A mixed heritage, a love of family, a love of country, and a political career that in just a few years has taken flight like few have seen or can comprehend, this is, in his words and the words of many others, the story in quotations of the life of Barack Obama.

On His Heritage

I was raised as an Indonesia child and a Hawaiian child and as a black child and as a white child. And so what I benefit from is a multiplicity of cultures that all fed me.[3]

I'm clear about my own identity. I do think that I've become a receptacle for a lot of other people's issues that they need to work out ... I've been living with this stuff my whole life.[4]

I've got relatives who look like Bernie Mac and I've got relatives who look like Margaret Thatcher. So we've got it all.[5]

In his speech at the Democratic National Convention in July 2004, Barack said, "My parents shared not only an improbable love; they shared an abiding faith in the possibilities of this nation. They would give me an African name, Barack, or 'blessed,' believing that in a tolerant America your name is no barrier to success."

Barack's father returned to Kenya when Barack was just two years old. In December 2007, Barack said that thoughts of his father would "bubble up," memories would come to him at different moments, at any course of the day or week. "I think about him often…. Men often long for their fathers' approval, to shine in their fathers' light." And when Barack Obama was asked how he feels about his father today, and asked what is the dominant emotion within these thoughts, he answered, "I didn't know him well enough to be angry at him as a father. Mostly I feel a certain sadness for him, and the way that his life ended up unfulfilled, despite his enormous talents."[6] About his father, Obama said,

> He was somebody who I think genuinely loved [his wife] but was also somebody who was more interested in his career and pursuing his ambitions, than he was caring for a family. [My mother] could have been bitter, but she didn't communicate that to me. She would talk about how smart he was, and how generous he was, and how charismatic he was, and for a little boy, that's actually a good thing…. Some of my drive comes from wanting to prove that he should have stuck around, that I was worthy of his attention.[7]

When Barack Obama visited his step-grandmother's compound on his first trip to Kenya, he said,

> It wasn't simply joy that I felt in each of these moments. Rather, it was a sense that everything I was doing, every touch and breath and word, carried the full weight of my life; that a circle was beginning to close, so that I might finally recognize myself as I was, here, now, in one place.[8]

After hearing the stories Obama said he felt dizzy with all of the new information about his father and his extended African family. All his life he had carried an image of his father. Barack Obama had not seen "his father shrunken or sick, his hopes ended or changed, his face full of regret or grief." It was his father's image, a black man from Africa, that he sought for himself and his father's voice remained "untainted, inspiring, rebuking, granting or withholding approval."[9]

Sarah Onyango Obama, Barack's Kenyan step-grandmother said, "I have had a dream you see, a recurring dream…. I have seen Barack surrounded by soldiers in dress uniform. At first I did not understand it, but now I realize it is because he is president." Sarah Obama added,

> Here we all believe education is the key ... his father had always talked about how well he was doing at school. When he came to stay with us the first time it must have been difficult, but he never let it show. He ate the same food as the rest of us, eggs, goat, sometimes fish.

Barack Obama's Kenyan uncle, Hussein Obama, said of Barack on his visit to Kenya: "We toured all the slums together. It was an eye-opening experience.... He is a role model and an achiever."[10]

Barack's mother, Stanley Ann Dunham Obama Soetoro, told Barack he should follow his father's example, that he had no choice because it was in his very genes. She said, "You have me to thank for your eyebrows ... but your brains, your character, you got from him." She brought home books on the civil rights movement, recordings of Mahalia Jackson, and the speeches of Martin Luther King. She told Barack stories of the schoolchildren in the south, and how although they had to read the books discarded by the white children, they went on to be successful doctors and lawyers. She added, "To be black was to be the beneficiary of a great inheritance, a special destiny, glorious burdens that only we were strong enough to bear."[11]

When Barack Obama was six years old, his mother married Lolo Soetoro, an Indonesian student at the University of Hawaii. Barack moved with his mother to Indonesia.

> I have wonderful memories of the place [Indonesia], but there's no doubt that, at some level, I understood that I was different. It meant that I was, maybe, not part of the community as much as I might have been, otherwise. On the other hand, it also gave me an appreciation of what it means to be an American.[12]

Barack turned to his stepfather, Lolo, for guidance and instruction. When Lolo explained the scars on his legs that came from the leeches that stuck to him as he and his fellow soldiers marched through the swamps in New Guinea, he told Barry (Barack's childhood name) that it hurt when the skin was singed after using a hot knife. He said, "Sometimes you can't worry about hurt. Sometimes you worry only about getting where you have to go." When he spoke of killing someone, he told Barry that he killed a man because the man was weak, and added, "Men take advantage of weakness in other men ... better to be strong ... if you can't be strong, be clever and make peace with someone who's strong ... but always better to be strong yourself. Always."[13]

Barack attended a Catholic school when he lived in Indonesia. His first grade teacher, Israella Pareira Darmawan, said, "He would be very helpful with friends. He'd pick them up if they fell down. He would protect the smaller ones."[14] Obama's third grade teacher said that in an essay about what he wanted to be when he grew up, Barack wrote that he wanted to be president. "He didn't say what country he wanted to be president of. But he wanted to make everybody happy."[15]

Barack Obama's boyhood experiences in Indonesia gave him a world view. He said in December 1995:

> The poverty, the corruption, the constant scramble for security ... remained all around me and bred a relentless skepticism. My mother's confidence in needlepoint virtues depended on a faith I didn't possess.... In a land where fatalism remained a necessary tool for enduring hard-ship ... she was a lonely witness for secular humanism, a soldier for New Deal, Peace Corps, position-paper liberalism.[16]

When Barack Obama was ten years old, his mother sent him back to Hawaii to live with her parents, deciding he needed to go to an American school. She stayed behind with Barack's half-sister, Maya, promising her young son that she and his sister would soon follow. Maya Soetoro-Ng said of Barack, their mother, and their grandparents,

> Looking back now, I'd say he really is kind of the perfect combination of all of them. All of them were imperfect but all of them loved him fiercely, and I believe he took the best qualities from each of them.[17]

Neil Abercrombie, a Democratic congressman from Hawaii who knew Barack Obama, his mother, and his grandparents, said of Stanley Dunham, Barack's grandfather, "Stanley loved that little boy. In the absence of his father, there was not a kinder, more understanding man than Stanley Dunham. He was loving and generous."[18]

After her divorce from Lolo Soetoro, Barack's mother returned to her studies at the University of Hawaii. She eventually returned to Indonesia to complete her fieldwork in anthropology, taking Maya with her. Barack stayed in Hawaii, choosing to remain with his grandparents and graduate from high school. Barack said of this arrangement: "I doubted what Indonesia now had to offer and wearied of being new all over again. More than that, I'd arrived at an unspoken pact with my grandparents: I could live with them and they'd leave me alone so long as I kept my trouble out of sight." Barack said during those years, he was "engaged in a fitful interior struggle. I was trying to raise myself to be a black man in America." Maya recalled her mother's quandary over leaving Barack in Hawaii:

> She wanted him to be with her. Although it was painful to be separated from him for his last four years of high school, she recognized that it was perhaps the best thing for him. And she had to go to Indonesia at that time ... There were certainly times in his life in those four years when he could have used her presence on a more daily basis. But I think he did all right for himself.[19]

Maya said of their mother, "She gave us a very broad understanding of the world. She hated bigotry. She was very determined to be remembered for a life of service and thought that service was really the true measure of a life."[20] Barack Obama said of being raised in a secular home:

> My mother saw religion as an impediment to broader values, like tolerance and racial inclusivity. She remembered church going folks [in Kansas and Texas] who also called people niggers. But she was a deeply spiritual person, and when I moved to Chicago [after graduating from Columbia] and worked with church-based community organizations, I kept hearing her values expressed in the church.[21]

Barack's half-sister, Maya, remembers Barack's high school days: "He had powers. He was charismatic. He had lots of friends. In high school, he used to stroll over to the Manoa campus of the University of Hawaii to 'meet university ladies.'"[22]

Obama's mother often wrote letters to her son about her life in Indonesia and her work there. She also sent him advice about his future, mixing encouragement with laments about American politics. She wrote in one of her letters:

> It is a shame we have to worry so much about [grade point], but you know what the college entrance competition is these days. Did you

know that in Thomas Jefferson's day, and right up through the 1930s, anybody who had the price of tuition could go to Harvard? I don't see that we are producing many Thomas Jeffersons nowadays. Instead we are producing Richard Nixons.[23]

Barack Obama remembered his mother this way:

> When I think about my mother, I think that there was a certain combination of being very grounded in who she was, what she believed in. But also a certain recklessness. I think she was always searching for something. She wasn't comfortable seeing her life confined in a certain box.[24]

Many of Barack Obama's mother's friends have seen much of Ann in Barack—in his self-assurance and drive, his boundary bridging, even his apparent comfort with strong women. One friend said, "When Barack smiles, there's just a certain *Ann* look. He lights up in a particular way that she did. There is this thing in his eyes."[25] Obama's mother died of ovarian cancer in 1995. Barack said of her:

> I think sometimes that had I known she would not survive her illness, I might have written a different book—less a meditation on the absent parent, more a celebration of the one who was the single constant in my life. I know that she was the kindest, most generous spirit I have ever known, and that what is best in me I owe to her.[26]

Nancy Barry, former president of Women's World Banking where Obama's mother worked in the early 1990s, said of Ann Obama Soetoro, "She was a very, very big thinker. I think she was not at all personally ambitious, I think she cared about the core issues, and I think she was not afraid to speak truth to power."[27]

Barack Obama says his mother taught him what she thought of as Midwestern, traditional American values—honesty, fairness, and plain speaking.

> She believed in saying what you mean and meaning what you say, even if it made a situation uncomfortable. To her that was part of her American tradition that she was proud of, and she wanted to make sure that was part of me.[28]

The dedication in his book *The Audacity of Hope* reads: "To the women who raised me—My maternal grandmother, Tutu, who's been a rock of stability throughout my life, and my mother, whose loving spirit sustains me still."[29]

Obama's half-sister, Maya, remembers their mother:

> She felt that somehow, wandering through uncharted territory, we might stumble upon something that will, in an instant, seem to represent who we are at the core. That was very much her philosophy of life—to not be limited by fear or narrow definitions, to not build walls around ourselves and to do our best to find kinship and beauty in unexpected places.[30]

David Axelrod, Obama's long-time friend and presidential campaign advisor said of Barack: "People measure experience in different ways. I think we're all an amalgam of all our experiences. And his are extremely varied and rich."[31]

On Marriage and Family

Throughout their marriage, as Obama made decisions in his political life, including his run for the Illinois state senate, when he made his first bid for the U.S. House of Representatives, when he decided to try again for national office by running for the open U.S. Senate seat, and before he decided to run for the 2008 presidency, there was always much to consider. He met with friends, his team of advisors, and tested the waters, but more important, he discussed such momentous decisions with Michelle.

On meeting Barack, Michelle Obama said she was ready to "write him off" before she first met him. "His name was Barack Obama, and I thought, 'Well, I'm sure this guy is weird, right?'" And when she learned he grew up in Hawaii and spent his formative years on an island, she thought, "Well, you've got to be a little nuts." Barack, she says, quickly changed her mind after their first conversation.[32]

Barack Obama said he was mesmerized by Michelle and vowed to go out on a date with her. According to her,

> He made the first move. I was skeptical at first; everyone was raving about this smart, attractive, young first-year associate they recruited from Harvard. Everyone was like, "Oh, he's brilliant, he's amazing

and he's attractive." I said, okay, this is probably just a Brother who can talk straight. Then I heard that he grew up in Hawaii. Weird background, so I said he's probably a little odd, strange. I already had in my mind that this guy was going to be lame. Then we went to lunch that first day and I was really impressed. First, he was more attractive than his picture. He came in confident, at ease with himself. He was easy to talk to and had a good sense of humor.

Michelle also says she was impressed with Barack's commitment to the community, yet for a month, she refused to go out with him.[33]

Barack has written candidly about the strains a political career has put on his marriage and his family.

> Leaning down to kiss Michelle goodbye in the morning, all I would get was a peck on the cheek. By the time Sasha was born—just as beautiful, and almost as calm as her sister—my wife's anger toward me seemed barely contained.[34]

Mutual respect is important to Michelle. She says of her husband:

> He's my biggest cheerleader, as a mother, as a wife and as a career person. He is always telling me how great I'm doing. That helps keep you going when you realize that you have someone who appreciates all the hard work that you are doing.[35]

Before Christmas 2006, Barack and Michelle met with their team of advisors to discuss throwing his hat in the ring. One of the advisors noted that, "He was very worried about what this was going to do to his family. I think Michelle at that point was very dubious, not at all enthusiastic about his running."[36]

As with most couples, the Obamas have weathered difficult times. Of the time just after their first daughter was born, Barack says:

> I was just getting into politics. There were a lot of stresses and strains. We didn't have a lot of money. I couldn't be as supportive of her at home as I wanted to be … but she knows how deeply I love her and the girls. I try to be more thoughtful. Sometimes it is just the little gestures that make a big difference.[37]

After thoroughly discussing the implications of his running for the presidency, Michelle had the final say on Barack throwing his hat into the presidential race. She said, "I never had a doubt about what Barack could offer, and that's what kind of spiraled me out of my own doubt. I don't want to be the person that holds back a potential answer to the nation's challenges." Of her husband's run for the presidency, Michelle said,

> It's important at this time for people to feel like they own this process and that they don't turn it over to the next messiah, who's going to fix it all, you know? And then we're surprised when people turn out not to be who we've envisioned them to be. There is specialness to him. If he's doing his job, he's going to say things that you don't agree with.[38]

The impact of a presidential race on his family concerned Barack; however, the opportunity of running for president proved to be irresistible. He said that what tipped the balance were the crowds.

> After seeing the response I was getting around the country, I had to step back and ask: Is there something about my message that is sufficiently unique and could potentially be useful enough to moving the country forward? And, ultimately, the answer was yes.[39]

Michelle had reservations about entering the campaign. She said,

> I, like most people, have been very cynical and reluctant about politics. You know, politics is a nasty business, and you don't hold out hope that fairness will win, that truth and justice carries the day. You think that it's a business. And there was a part of me that said "Do we want to put ourselves out for a system that I am not sure about?" What Barack and I talked about when we decided to do this was that we were going to do this authentically and that this was as much a test for us about the country and the (political) process as it was the other way around ... if you offer somebody what is real and true, will people grasp that? I want to believe they will, because that's what they've got in front of them.[40]

Michelle said, "You know, Barack is very convincing and very passionate," adding that she was naïve in the beginning about the impact it would have on their family life, "So I eventually said: 'Sure, let's do it. Okay you win.' And then, you're in."[41] Michelle defended her husband against claims he shouldn't be running in 2008:

> Don't be fooled by people who claim that it is not his time. We've heard this spewed from the lips of rivals … every phase of our journey: He is not experienced enough. He should wait his turn. He is too young. He is not black enough. He is not white enough … you win with being who you are and with being clear and comfortable with that. I'm finding that people completely understand me. For the most part, I think the women and the men and the families and the folks that we are meeting on the campaign trail understand the realities of families of today.[42]

Michelle, however, likes to remind audiences her husband is just a man—at once extraordinary and quite ordinary—a man who forgets to pick up his socks. She wants to humanize her husband many see as the "Great Black Hope." Michelle said,

> I know that I can't do it all. I cannot be involved in a presidential campaign, hold down a full-time senior-level position, get my kids to camp, and exercise and eat right. I know I can't do it all. So forgive me for being human, but I'm going to put it on the table. You've got to make trade-offs in life. I'm okay with that. I've come to realize I am sacrificing one set of things in my life for something else potentially really positive.

On the campaign for the presidency, Michelle said,

> I'm here not just because I'm the wife of a candidate. Because this is hard. This is really a hard thing. This isn't a natural choice to be made in your life. It's strange, all this. I'm here as a woman, as a mother, as a citizen of this country. And I am so tired of the way things are.[43]

After Barack Obama's announcement that he would seek the presidency, many speculated about his chances of winning the nomination, to say nothing of his chances for winning the general election. Many secretly and openly were concerned about his safety. On this, Michelle said,

I tell myself all the time, we're supposed to take the risk. In the end, I think we have an obligation to give it a shot. To do our best. To give people a choice ... I took myself down every dark road you could go on, just to prepare myself before we jumped out there. Are we emotionally, financially ready for this? I dreamed out all the scenarios. The bottom line is, man, the little sacrifice we have to make is nothing compared to the possibility of what we could do if this catches on.[44]

For much of the year, Barack is away from home, and the time away comes with some strife in the Obama household. Michelle said,

Sundays once were sacred in the Obama house, the day for school activities and reading, movies and catching up on writing in the family journal. But in the final months of the year, Obama's political schedule began filling up ... the hope is that this is going to change and we're going to go back to our normal schedule of keeping Sundays pretty sacred.[45]

For many years, Barack attended the Trinity United Church of Christ in Chicago, Illinois. It is the church where he and Michelle were married, where his two daughters were baptized, and whose pastor blessed the Obama home. The church's former pastor, Jeremiah A. Wright, said of Barack, "His wife and his daughters come before his political career and that is crucial in a time when families are coming apart."[46]

Barack and his family have a tradition of taking a family vacation to visit family and friends in Hawaii. While serving in the Illinois state senate, an important senate vote was scheduled while Barack and his family were on their annual trip; he could not make it back to Springfield in time for the vote, in part because of one of his daughters being too sick to fly home. Barack missed the vote and the consequences were often noted during his time in the state senate and also during his campaigns for national office. Barack said of missing the vote and the resulting consequences:

I take my legislative responsibilities extremely seriously. In the midst of a congressional race, I'm well aware of the potential risk of missing a vote, even if that vote doesn't wind up making the difference on a particular piece of legislation. But at some point, family has to come first.[47]

Michelle says of her husband that he's not the "next messiah, who's going to fix it all. He is going to stumble ... make mistakes and say things you don't agree with." When asked what happens when her husband wants her input on policy issues, her reply is, "Do you think I would ever hold my tongue?"[48]

When asked about the race and being in the White House, Michelle said, "My God, who can sit here and say, 'I'm ready to be president and first lady?' " In regard to the rigors of the campaign trail, Michelle said, "I wake up every morning wondering how on the earth I am going to pull off that next minor miracle of getting through the day."[49]

Spending the July 4th holiday on the campaign trail in Iowa, Barack said, "This is the family weekend for us." As the family loaded up into

Democratic presidential nominee Senator Barack Obama arrives for an election night rally with his wife Michelle in St. Paul, Minnesota on June 3, 2008. (AP Photo/Chris Carlson)

a recreational vehicle heading for another campaign stop, he added, "Family is first."[50]

Barack Obama reflected on his father and his own fatherhood:

> I think that, both consciously and unconsciously, it's been helpful for me to understand the mistakes that my father made. I think a lot about trying to spend enough time with my kids. I think a lot about not being too heavy-handed with my children. I think about the importance of showing respect to my wife as part of showing love and regard for my kids … the approval that I desire now is the approval of my kids. It's an interesting turn in my life, where I'm much more concerned about whether my 9-year-old and 6-year-old think I'm a good dad, than that crowd of 5,000 people that are cheering me on.[51]

Barack's daughter Malia, has said, "Are you going to try to be president? Shouldn't you be vice president first?"[52]

NOTES

1. Christine Brozyna, "Get to Know Barack Obama," *ABC News,* November 2, 2007.
2. Nicholas D. Kristof, "Obama: Man of the World," *New York Times,* March 6, 2007, A.21.
3. David Mendell, *Obama: From Promise to Power* (New York: Amistad, 2007), 32.
4. Eugene Robinson, "The Moment for This Messenger?" *Washington Post,* March 13, 2007, A17.
5. Steve Dougherty, *Hopes and Dreams: The Story of Barack Obama* (New York: Black Dog & Leventhal Publishers, Inc., 2007), 44.
6. Kevin Merida, "The Ghost of a Father," *Washington Post,* December 4, 2007, A12.
7. Brozyna, "Get to Know Barack Obama."
8. Barack Obama, *Dreams from My Father* (New York: Three Rivers Press, 2004), 376–377.
9. Ibid., 220.
10. Jonathan Clayton and Nyangoma Korela, "Favourite Son is Already a Winner in Kenya," *Times of London,* February 10, 2007, http://www.timesoflondon.com (accessed February 10, 2007).
11. Obama, *Dreams from My Father,* 50–51.
12. Brozyna, "Get to Know Barack Obama."
13. Obama, *Dreams from My Father,* 36–41.
14. Kirsten Scharnberg and Kim Barker, "The Not-So-Simple Story of Barack Obama's Youth," *Chicago Tribune Online Edition,* March 25, 2007, http://www.chicagotribune.com (accessed March 25, 2007).
15. Ibid.
16. Hank De Zutter, "What Makes Obama Run?" *Chicago Reader,* December 8, 1995, http://www.chicagoreader.com (accessed June 3, 2008).

17. Scharnberg and Barker, "Not-So-Simple Story of Barack Obama's Youth."
18. Ibid.
19. Janny Scott, "A Free-Spirited Wanderer Who Set Obama's Path," *New York Times,* March 14, 2008, http://www.nytimes.com (accessed March 14, 2008).
20. Ibid.
21. Jonathan Alter and Daren Briscoe, "The Audacity of Hope," *Newsweek,* December 27, 2004, 74–87.
22. Amanda Ripley, David E. Thigpen, and Jeannie McCabe, "Obama's Ascent," *Time,* November 15, 2004, 74–81.
23. Scharnberg and Barker, "Not-So-Simple Story of Barack Obama's Youth."
24. Amanda Ripley, "A Mother's Story," *Time,* April 21, 2008, 36, 39.
25. Ibid., 42.
26. Scott, "A Free-Spirited Wanderer Who Set Obama's Path."
27. Ibid.
28. Richard Wolffe, Jessica Ramirez, and Jeffrey Bartholet, "When Barry Became Barack," *Newsweek,* March 22, 2008, http://www.newsweek.com (accessed March 24, 2008).
29. Barack Obama, *The Audacity of Hope* (New York: Crown Publishers, 2006).
30. Scott, "A Free-Spirited Wanderer Who Set Obama's Path."
31. Jackie Calmes, "Politics & Economics: Democrats' Litmus Electability," *Wall Street Journal,* January 11, 2007, A.6.
32. Beverly Wang, "Michelle Obama Says Husband Has Moral Compass," *Associated Press,* 7 May 2007.
33. Lynn Norment, "The Hottest Couple in America," *Ebony,* February 1, 2007, 52.
34. Karen Tumulty, "The Real Running Mates," *Time,* September 24, 2007, 35.
35. Norment, "The Hottest Couple in America."
36. Liza Mundy, "A Series of Fortunate Events," *Washington Post,* August 12, 2007, W10.
37. Norment, "The Hottest Couple in America."
38. Judy Keen, "Candid and Unscripted, Campaigning Her Way," *USA Today,* May 11, 2007, 01a.
39. Mundy, "A Series of Fortunate Events."
40. Michele Norris, "Michelle Obama Sees Election as Test for America," *National Public Radio,* July 9, 2007, http://www.npr.org (accessed July 9, 2007).
41. Mundy, "A Series of Fortunate Events."
42. Tumulty, "The Real Running Mates."
43. Gwen Ifill, "On the Road with Michelle Obama," *Essence,* September 7, 2007, 204.
44. Ibid., 206.
45. Jeff Zeleny, "The First Time Around: Senator Obama's Freshman Year," *Chicago Tribune,* December 24, 2005, http://www.chicagotribune.com/news/local/chi-051224obama,0,6232648.story (accessed May 20, 2008).
46. Dougherty, *Hopes and Dreams.*
47. Peter Slevin, "Obama Forged Political Mettle in Illinois Capitol," *Washington Post,* February 9, 2007, A01.

48. Judy Keen, "Candid and Unscripted, Campaigning Her Way," *USA Today,* May 11, 2007, 01a.

49. Jodi Kantor and Jeff Zeleny, "Michelle Obama Adds New Role to Balancing Act," *New York Times,* May 18, 2007, A1.

50. "Obama Says He Is Emissary for Change," *Associated Press,* July 5, 2007, http://www.msnbc.msn.com (accessed July 5, 2007).

51. Brozyna, "Get to Know Barack Obama."

52. Dougherty, *Hopes and Dreams,* 114.

CHAPTER 2

On Community Organizing and Activism and Accepting the Call to Serve

"Organizing teaches as nothing else does the beauty and strength of everyday people. Through the songs of the church and the talk on the stoops, through the hundreds of individual stories of coming up from the South and finding any job that would pay, of raising families on threadbare budgets, of losing some children to drugs and watching others earn degrees and land jobs their parents could never aspire to—it is through these stories and songs of dashed hopes and powers of endurance, of ugliness and strife, subtlety and laughter, that organizers can shape a sense of community not only for others, but for themselves."[1]

Introduction

In 1983, ready to graduate from Columbia University, Barack made the decision to pursue a career in community activism, even though he knew no one making a living as an activist, nor did he know what such a job's duties might be. Change, Barack knew, happened at the grassroots level, and he wanted to organize people to effect change. Living in New York at the time, Barack wrote letters to every civil rights organization he could think of. He wrote to elected black officials, and to neighborhood councils and tenants' rights groups. Receiving no response, he decided to accept a job to save money and pay off school debt. After a time, the idea of community organizing still tugged at him, and he quit his position, determined to find another in his chosen field. Writing more letters and receiving no response, after six months, he remained unemployed. He had nearly given up when he received a call from a community organizer in Chicago. He needed a trainee, the man said, someone that could join urban blacks and suburban whites in the Chicago area in an attempt to save manufacturing jobs. The job offer included a salary and a travel allowance that Barack used to buy a car. Barack moved to Chicago, a place he had visited years before with his mother and grandmother. For three years, he drove his battered Honda Civic to church and neighborhood meetings in an effort to effect changes. There were successes and failures; however, Barack kept at it with a positive outlook, determination, and a drive to succeed. He was twenty-four years old and doing what he felt he needed to do. Barack has often said that his time on the south side of Chicago as a community organizer was the best education possible. Community organizing and activism had a profound impact on how Barack approached politics, his views on issues, and his connection to people.

On Community Organizing and Activism

On his decision to become a community activist, Barack said,

> The idea of being part of a community, and helping build that community, was very appealing to me, and very attractive to me. I think that being part of an African-American community was also

important to me, because I think I felt there was a strong gravitational pull, given I had graduated from an Ivy League school to go into a rarefied world in which I wouldn't really be rooted in a particular community. And that was something I wanted to avoid.[2]

Just out of college and unable to find a position as a community activist, Barack accepted a position as a research assistant at a consulting house to multinational corporations in New York. Of the time there, he wrote,

> Sometimes, coming out of an interview with Japanese financiers or German bond traders, I would catch my reflection in the elevator doors—see myself in a suit and tie, a briefcase in my hand—and for a split second I would imagine myself as a captain of industry, barking out orders, closing the deal, before I remembered who it was that I had told myself I wanted to be and felt pangs of guilt for my lack of resolve.[3]

Barack's supervisor at the consulting firm, Cathy Lazere, has said, "He was very mature and more worldly than other people—on the surface kind of laid back, but kind of in control. He had a good sense of himself, which I think a lot of kids at that age don't."[4]

Determined to become a community organizer, Barack sent letters to everyone he knew and to every organization he knew of that were doing what he wanted to do. His only response came from Gerald Kellman of the Developing Communities Project (DCP) in Chicago. After meeting with Kellman, Barack was offered a position and moved to Chicago.

Gerald Kellman said of Barack's training as a community organizer in Chicago, "We did training in listening skills ... you're listening for story, because story communicates more about a person than simply facts.... Barack did that very well. One of the remarkable things is how well he listens to people who are opposed to him."[5]

In community activism, Barack was looking for an authentic African American experience. Gerald Kellman and his DCP were searching for an authentic African American to work in the black neighborhoods that had been devastated by the closing of the factories and mills on the south side of Chicago. Barack's job sent him to the poor black neighborhoods where he knew he wanted to make a connection. It was also a

Democratic presidential candidate Senator Barack Obama waves to the media as he leaves the Democratic National Committee headquarters in June 2008. (AP Photo/Jose Luis Magana)

job where he worked with area churches to effect community changes. From the church leaders, Barack soon learned that the difficulty he was having in enabling and effecting the grassroots changes and earning the trust and commitment from the churches was because he wasn't showing up in the church pews on Sunday. When meeting with pastors in area churches, he was asked about his own spiritual life. One of the pastors said,

> It might help your mission if you had a church home. It doesn't matter where, really. What you're asking from pastors requires us to set aside some of our more priestly concerns in favor of prophesy. That requires a good deal of faith on our part. It makes us want to know just where you're getting yours from.

After lectures like this, Barack visited the Trinity United Church of Christ. The church's pastor, Reverend Jeremiah Wright, became Barack's pastor, a mentor, and much later on in Barack's life while in the midst of the presidential campaign, his former pastor. The church helped Barack develop as a community organizer and also to develop politically.[6]

When Barack submitted his first report of interviews, his supervisor, Gerald Kellman said, "You're starting to listen.... But, it's still too abstract ... if you want to organize people ... go towards people's centers ... what makes them tick ... form the relationships you need to get them involved."[7]

Kellman said his sense was that Barack's dream after Harvard Law School was to come back to Chicago and possibly become mayor of Chicago. Barack said this never occurred to him at the time, saying,

> I was, like many people, impressed by the degree to which he [Harold Washington, mayor of Chicago, who died of a heart attack while in office], could mobilize the community and push for change.... I was somewhat disdainful of politics. I was much more interested in mobilizing people to hold politicians accountable.[8]

In October 2004, Barack was asked how he assessed the impact of having been a community organizer on choosing politics as a career. He answered,

> I became a community organizer as a direct result of my work and study in college. I was greatly inspired by the civil rights movement ... my coming back to Chicago, I think, opened up my potential—I consider [the experience] an extension of my college education because a lot of the things that I had read about in books I had to try to implement. It wasn't always as easy as I thought, but it also confirmed my belief in the need to give everyday folks a handle on their own destiny. And all my work since that time has been shaped by the values that were forged during those years as a community organizer.[9]

In a speech to the National Action Network (NAN), a civil rights group founded by Al Sharpton, Barack touted his experience as a community organizer and state senator from Illinois as examples of his experience and leadership ability. He said, "I haven't just talked about these things, I've actually done them."[10]

Of his time as a community organizer in Chicago, Michael Evans of the DCP remembers Barack saying "You can only go so far in organizing. You help people get some solutions, but it's never as big as wiping away problems. It wasn't end-all. He wanted to be part of the end-all, to get things done."[11]

In Chicago, Barack spoke to a number of black ministers to persuade them to ally themselves with the DCP. He discovered that most of these ministers had something in common.

> One minister talked about a former gambling addiction. Another told me about his years as a successful executive and a secret drunk. They all mentioned periods of religious doubt ... the striking bottom and shattering of pride; and then finally the resurrection of self, a self alloyed to something larger. That was the source of their confidence, they insisted: their personal fall, their subsequent redemption. It was what gave them the authority to preach the Good News.[12]

Another member of the DCP in Chicago, Loretta Augustine-Herron, said of Barack that he was "Someone who always followed the high road," and remembered him saying,

> [Y]ou've got to do it right ... be open with the issues ... include the community instead of going behind the community's back, and that he would include people we didn't like sometimes ... you've got to bring people together. If you exclude people, you're only weakening yourself. If you meet behind doors and make decisions for them, they'll never take ownership of the issue.[13]

Reverend Alvin Love, who was recruited to participate in the DCP, looks at Barack's candidacy and says, "Everything I see reflects that community organizing experience ... consensus-building ... connection to people ... listening ... common ground. I think at his heart Barack is a community organizer ... what he's doing now is that. It's just a larger community to be organized."[14] Pastor Love spoke of the young Barack:

> Barack kind of broke down those barriers for us, because it was easy for us to get into our own agenda. And it was all the neighborhoods

on the South Side, and all the pastors were saying the same thing, so finding out that we had more in common than we thought was an eye-opening experience." Love said Barack was a stubborn, "stiff-necked grinder with a gift for changing tactics on the fly.

Recalling a first meeting at Altgeld Gardens, a housing project on the South Side of Chicago, that didn't go well, Love said,

[A]n arrogant city bureaucrat got everybody's back up … half the people wanted to walk out, and the other half wanted to deck the guy.… Barack wouldn't quit. He pulled us off to the side and he said, "Well, we messed that up. We didn't see that coming. We need to strategize right now about how to deal with stuff like this and hold people accountable so this kind of thing doesn't happen again."[15]

At a DCP convention in 2004, Barack told the members,

I can't say we didn't make mistakes, that I knew what I was doing. Sometimes I called a meeting, and nobody showed up. Sometimes preachers said, "Why should I listen to you?" Sometimes we tried to hold politicians accountable, and they didn't show up. I couldn't tell whether I got more out of it than this neighborhood. I grew up to be a man, right here, in this area. It's a consequence of working with this organization and this community that I found my calling. There was something more than making money and getting a fancy degree. The measure of my life would be public service.[16]

Barack's work on the south side of Chicago won him many friendships and the respect of fellow activists. One friendship was with Johnnie Owens, who left the citywide advocacy group Friends of the Parks to join Barack at the DCP. When Barack left Chicago to attend Harvard Law School, Owens replaced Barack as the executive director of DCP. He said of Barack:

What I liked about Barack immediately is that he brought a certain level of sophistication and intelligence to community work. He had a reasonable, focused approach that I hadn't seen much of. A lot of organizers you meet these days are these self-anointed leaders with this strange, way-out approach and unrealistic, eccentric way of pursuing things from the very beginning. Not Barack. He's not about calling attention to himself. He's concerned with the work. It's as if it's his mission in life, his calling, to work for social justice. Anyone who knows me knows that I'm one of the most cynical people you want to see, always looking for somebody's angle or personal interest. I've lived in Chicago all my life. I've known some of the most ruthless and biggest bullshitters out there, but I see nothing but integrity in this guy.[17]

Senator Hillary Clinton has criticized Barack on his lack of experience and his qualifications to be president. In response, Barack said the following in July 2007:

What I know is the kind of experience I have outside of Washington as a community organizer working with families that are struggling, as a constitutional law professor, as a state legislator dealing with the very issues that affect people, people find that experience at least as relevant, maybe more relevant, than experience in Washington.[18]

On Barack's experience, Michelle Obama said, "We've defined 'experience' very narrowly," citing her husband's years of community organizing in Chicago, his experience in the Illinois state senate and U.S. Senate, and his expertise as a civil-rights attorney and constitutional law scholar.

He probably knows the Constitution better than this administration. This is probably the only country on earth that would look at somebody like Barack Obama and his more than 25 years of public service, and say that he's not experienced. That's the irony of it. That's the game of politics.[19]

Barack posted this message on his website regarding forming a presidential exploratory committee: "Years ago, as a community organizer in Chicago, I learned that meaningful change always begins at the grassroots, and that engaged citizens working together can accomplish extraordinary things."[20]

On a phone conference call in June 2007, Barack told organizers preparing to go door-to-door for his campaign, "I was a community organizer on the south side of Chicago, doing a lot of the work that a lot of you guys are going to do on Saturday. You may get some doors slammed in your face or people arguing with you." The important thing, he added, "is to listen."[21]

In a speech following the Iowa Caucuses on January 3, 2008, Barack told the huge crowd that they didn't do it for him. Instead, they did it because they believed deeply in the most American of ideas.

> I know this. I know this because while I may be standing here tonight, I'll never forget that my journey began on the streets of Chicago doing what so many of you have done for this campaign and all the campaigns here in Iowa, organizing and working and fighting to make people's lives just a little bit better.[22]

> Though I'm clearly a political leader now, I didn't start as one. I was skeptical of electoral politics. I thought it was corrupting, and that real change would happen in the grass roots.... I thought the way to have an impact was through changing people's hearts and minds, not through some government program.[23]

In 1995, Barack was running to be the Democratic candidate for the Illinois state senate from the south side of Chicago. The *Chicago Reader* wrote about him as a lawyer, teacher, philanthropist, and author, noting that although he didn't need yet another career, he found one in politics to get to his true passion—community organization. Barack said the following in the article:

> What if a politician were to see his job as that of an organizer, as part teacher and part advocate, one who does not sell voters short but who educates them about the real choices before them? As an elected public official, for instance, I could bring church and community leaders together easier than I could as a community organizer or lawyer. We would come together to form concrete economic development strategies, take advantage of existing laws and structures, and create bridges and bonds within all sectors of the community. We must form grass-root structures that would hold me and other elected officials more accountable for their actions.[24]

Vernon Jordan, Barack's friend and President Clinton's advisor, has said, "I am just very impressed with him as a man, as a lawyer, as an individual, and as someone who chose not to go to a law firm but to be a community organizer and to do something about community problems."[25]

On Accepting the Call to Serve

The first time many people heard of Barack Obama was at the Democratic National Convention in 2004. He stood at the podium, in front of thousands of Democrats, and spoke. The speech that night, one he'd written himself and delivered without using a teleprompter, electrified the Democrats before him, and amazed and inspired those who watched on television. It also amazed the millions who heard about it for days on end. Although the whole of the speech was stirring, the words that follow perhaps speak to what Barack believes about his service to the country and accepting the call to serve at this point in his life: "I stand here knowing that my story is part of the larger American story, that I owe a debt to all of those who came before me, and that in no other country on earth is my story even possible." With a fervor that could be felt by all who were there and all who were watching, Barack went on:

> Tonight we gather to affirm the greatness of our nation, not because of the height of our skyscrapers or the power of our military or the size of our economy. Our pride is based on a very simple premise, summed up in a declaration made over 200 years ago: "We hold these truths to be self-evident, that all men are created equal."[26]

Speaking to a group of college students in Washington, D.C. in July 2006, Barack said,

> You'll have boundless opportunities when you graduate and it's very easy to just take that diploma, forget about all this progressive-politics stuff, and go chasing after the big house and the large salary and the nice suits and all the other things that our money culture says you should buy. But I hope you don't get off that easy. There's nothing wrong with making money, but focusing your life solely on making a buck shows a poverty of ambition.

On an American culture that "discourages empathy," and belief that "innocent people being slaughtered and expelled from their homes halfway around the world are somebody else's problem," Barack urged the group of college students to ignore those voices:

> [Not] because you have an obligation to those who are less fortunate than you, although I think you do have that obligation, but primarily because you have that obligation to yourself. Because our individual salvation depends on collective salvation. It's only when you hitch yourself up to something bigger than yourself that you realize your true potential.[27]

On how his experience as a law professor shaped him as a political leader, Barack responded:

> One of the things that an effective professor learns is how to present both sides of an argument ... and I think that being able to see all sides of an issue, having been trained in presenting all sides of an issue in the classroom, actually helps me question my own assumptions and helps me empathize with people who don't agree with me.[28]

Barack announced he was forming a presidential exploratory committee and posted this message on his website:

> I certainly didn't expect to find myself in this position a year ago. I've been struck by how hungry we all are for a different kind of politics. So I've spent some time thinking about how I could best advance the cause of change and progress that we so desperately need.[29]

Announcing his candidacy in February 2007 in Springfield, Illinois, Barack said, "Each and very time, a new generation has risen up and done what's needed to be done. Today we are called once more, and it is time for our generation to answer that call." To the crowd in Springfield Barack added, "That is why this campaign can't only be about me. It must be about us. It must be about what we can do together."[30]

On community and shared sacrifice, Barack said, "We have responsibilities to ourselves, but we also have mutual responsibilities, so if a child can't read so well, that matters to us even if they are not our child." When asked by a woman if her son's death in Iraq was the result of a mistake by the government, Barack answered, "I told her the service of our young men and women—the duty they show this country—that's never a mistake." Afterwards, he reflected on the encounter: "It reminds you why you get into politics. It reminds you that this isn't a game."[31]

When speaking to a group of African American political organizers in New York, Barack said he did not want black votes simply because he was black: "That's not what America is about. I want it to be because of what I've done, and how I've lived, and the principles I stand for, and the ideas I promote."[32]

Valerie Jarrett, a family friend for many years, said the following of Barack:

He's always wanted to be president. He didn't always admit it, but oh, absolutely. The first time he said to me, he said, "I just think I have some special qualities and wouldn't it be a shame to waste them." I think it was during the early part of his U.S. senatorial campaign. He said, "You know, I just think I have something."

In Iowa, prior to the Iowa Caucus in January 2008, Barack said,

Some people who knew of my activism in the community asked me would I be interested in running for that office. And so I did what every wise man does when confronted with such a decision: I prayed on it, and I asked my wife.[33]

When asked whether he believed that God took sides in a war, Barack quoted Abraham Lincoln, and then added that it was important to remain "our brother's keeper, our sister's keeper" to advance the causes of justice and freedom.[34]

Barack noted:

One sort of measure of my own wisdom is the degree to which I can clear my mind of ego and focus on what's useful, and I'm not always successful at that. I'm subject like everyone else to vanity and what Dr. [Martin Luther] King called "the drum major instinct" of wanting to lead the parade."[35]

In Reno, Nevada, to a crowd described as large, passionate, and politically diverse, Barack said the current philosophy in Washington is that "if you are a child that didn't have the wisdom to choose the right parents you're on your own," and then called for a new, less selfish, less timid politics that "reflects the core decency of the American people."[36]

State of Illinois Senator Kirk Dillard, a Republican who befriended Barack during his term as a state senator, said,

Obama has a great intellect and the leadership characteristics of our great American presidents. But the unknown is the administrative and foreign policy experience.... I would not lose a night's sleep worrying about my young children's future if Senator Obama were my president because I know he would probably surround himself, like Ronald Reagan, with exceptionally experienced people.[37]

Writing in the journal *Foreign Affairs,* Barack said,

Today, we are again called to provide visionary leadership. This century's threats are at least as dangerous as and in some ways more complex than those we have confronted in the past.

It is a call to action. These threats demand a new vision of leadership in the twenty-first century—a vision that draws from the past but is not bound by outdated thinking ... the world has lost trust in our purposes and our principles.

America cannot meet the threats of this century alone, and the world cannot meet them without America. We can neither retreat from the world nor try to bully it into submission. We must lead the world, by deed and by example.

The American moment is not over, but it must be seized anew. To see American power in terminal decline is to ignore America's great promise and historic purpose in the world.

This is our moment to renew the trust and faith of our people—and all people—in an America that battles immediate evils, promotes an ultimate good, and leads the world once more.[38]

When speaking about misperceptions, Michelle Obama said the following of Barack:

Barack poses this interesting dilemma because we are still a country that puts people in boxes. Barack kind of shakes up those notions because his life has crossed so many different paths. He grew up in Hawaii but he was indeed a community organizer. He became very entrenched and rooted in the black community on the South Side [of Chicago]. He is very much a black man, but he's very much the son of his mother, who was very much a white woman, and he grew up with white grandparents.[39]

On Barack's swift rise in the polls and his sudden intense popularity, "It's like he cut in line. He's become a household name far faster than anyone who doesn't have a hit movie," said Tony Bullock, vice president of Ogilvy Public Relationships Worldwide and former Hill staffer.[40]

Donna Brazile, a Democratic political consultant, said, "He became an important person overnight. What's unusual is that most political celebrities—Hillary Clinton, Al Gore, John McCain—earn that status only after prolonged ordeals. What's unique about Obama is that he's done it because he's cool. Because he's new."[41]

In September 2007, Barack said, "One of the dangers of movements is that they always want to be completely pure and have everything their way. But politics is about governing and making compromises. And so sometimes folks who come into politics with a movement mentality can be disappointed."[42]

An old friend of Barack's said in September 2007, "You don't get to where Obama is by being Mr. Goodie every day. You do have to compromise your values."[43]

In a speech at DePaul University on October 2, 2007, Barack said,

I want to be straight with you. If you want conventional Washington thinking, I'm not your man. If you want rigid ideology, I'm not your man. If you think that fundamental change can wait, I'm definitely not your man. But if you want to bring this country together, if you want experience that's broader than just learning the ways of Washington, if you think that the global challenges we face are too urgent to wait, and if you think that America must offer the world a new and hopeful face, then I offer a different choice in this race and a different vision for our future.[44]

At the same speech, Barack said,

In the 21st century, we cannot stand up before the world and say that there's one set of rules for America and another for everyone else. To lead the world, we must lead by example. We must be willing to acknowledge our failings, not just trumpet our victories.[45]

David Bartholomew, a law student at Boston College Law School said in November 2007 that Barack is "a citizen of the world. Obama and my generation—we see the future of the world as countries evolving together. Because of his background he can speak to a wider range of people than any other candidate. He can speak globally."[46]

In a speech at the Jefferson-Jackson dinner in Iowa in November 2007, Barack said,

I don't want to spend the next year or the next 4 years refighting the same fights that we had in the 1990s. In this election—at this moment—let us reach for what we know is possible. A nation healed. A world repaired. An America that believes again.[47]

In an interview with *Time*, in regard to National Service, and asking all of the nation's youth to serve their country in some capacity, whether it is the Peace Corp, the military, or in some other way, Barack said, "I can make government and public service cool again."[48]

On judgment and experience, Barack said in December 2007, "People want judgment, and they hope that experience is often a good proxy.... Experience can actually be an impediment to good judgment."[49]

On a long and brutal campaign season, Barack believes the exercise is a good one for picking the next president of the United States:

Ultimately, the process reveals aspects of an individual's character and judgment. If you think about past Presidents, probably those two things along with vision are the most important aspects of a presidency. Do you know where you want to take the country? Do you have the judgment to figure out what's important and what's not? Do you have the character to withstand trials and tribulations and to bounce back from setbacks?"[50]

After the New Hampshire Primary, where it was expected, according to the polls, that Barack would win the contest, and where Hillary Clinton won after she and her campaign were nearly written off, Barack strode onstage at Nashua (New Hampshire) South High School, and conceded defeat. "I am still fired up and ready to go.... We've been told we're not ready, that we shouldn't try, or that we can't, and generations of Americans have responded with a simple creed that sums up the spirit of a people: Yes, we can."[51]

After the February 12th Chesapeake primaries, Barack spoke to the gathered crowd of supporters and said,

> The voices of the American people have carried us a great distance on this improbable journey, but we have much further to go. Now we carry our message ... it's the same message we had when we were up, and when were down; that out of many, we are one; that our destiny will not be written for us, but by us; and that we can cast off our doubts and fears and cynicism because our dream will not be deferred; our future will not be denied; and our time for change has come.[52]

In a speech on race on March 19, 2008, Barack said,

> We have a choice in this country: we can accept a politics that breeds division, and conflict, and cynicism. Or, at this moment, in this election, we can come together and say: "not this time"... and today, whenever I find myself feeling doubtful or cynical about this possibility, what gives me the most hope is the next generation: the young people whose attitudes and beliefs and openness to change have already made history in this election.[53]

According to David Axelrod, the Obama campaign's chief strategist, the bottom-up ethos of the campaign comes straight from the top:

> When we started this race, Barack told us that he wanted the campaign to be a vehicle for involving people and giving them a stake in the kind of organizing he believes in. He is still the same guy who came to Chicago as a community organizer twenty-three years ago. The idea that we can organize together and improve our country—I mean, he really believes that.[54]

On May 25, 2008, Barack delivered the commencement address at Wesleyan University in Middletown, Connecticut. Encouraging community service and service to country, he said,

> You are about to enter a world that makes it easy to get caught up in the notion that there are actually two different stories at work in our

lives. The first is the story of our everyday cares and concerns—the responsibilities we have to our jobs and our families … and the second is the story of what happens in the life of our country—of what happens in the wider world. It's the story you see when you catch a glimpse of the day's headlines or turn on the news at night—a story of big challenges like war and recession; hunger and climate change; injustice and inequality. It's a story that can sometimes seem distant and separate from our own—a destiny to be shaped by forces beyond our control.… I say this to you as someone who couldn't be standing here today if not for the service of others, and wouldn't be standing here today if not for the purpose that service gave my own life … each of us can do our part … our collective service can shape the destiny of this generation … that is all I ask of you on this joyous day of new beginnings … that is how we will keep so much needed work going, and the cause of justice everlasting, and the dream alive for generations to come.[55]

Barack said the following at Indiana's Jefferson–Jackson Dinner on May 4, 2008:

When I began this campaign for the presidency, I said I was running because I believed that the size of our challenges had outgrown the smallness of our politics in Washington—the pettiness and the game-playing and the influence-peddling that always prevents us from solving the problems we face year after year after year.… I also saw that we are not powerless in the face of these challenges. We don't have to sit here and watch our leaders do nothing.… And that's why I'm running because we can't afford to settle for a Washington where John McCain gets the chance to give us four more years of the same.… We can't afford to settle for a Washington where politicians only focus on how to win instead of why we should; where they check the polls before they check their gut; where they only tell us whatever we want to hear whenever we want to hear it. That kind of politics may get them where they need to go, but it doesn't get America where we need to go. And it won't change anything.… It's about who we are as Americans. It's about whether this country, at this moment, will continue to stand by while the wealthy few prosper at the expense of the hardworking many, or whether we'll stand up and reclaim the American dream for every American.[56]

On the evening of the North Carolina Primary, May 6, 2008, Barack said the following:

> [B]ecause you still believe that this is our moment, and our time, for change … that we are at our best when we lead with principle; when we lead with conviction; when we summon an entire nation around a common purpose—a higher purpose … we also believe we have a larger responsibility to one another as Americans—that America is a place—that America is the place—where you can make it if you try. That no matter how much money you start with or where you come from or who your parents are, opportunity is yours if you're willing to reach for it and work for it … not what kind of campaign they'll run, it's what kind of campaign we will run. It's what we will do to make this year different. I didn't get into [this] race thinking that I could avoid this kind of politics, but I am running for president because this is the time to end it…. We will end it by telling the truth—forcefully, repeatedly, confidently—and by trusting that the American people will embrace the need for change … that's how we've always changed this country—not from the top-down, but from the bottom-up; when you—the American people—decide that the stakes are too high and the challenges are too great…. That's why I'm in this race. I love this country too much to see it divided and distracted at this moment in history. I believe in our ability to perfect this union because it's the only reason I'm standing here today. And I know the promise of America because I have lived it … this election is not about me, or any candidate. Don't ever forget that this campaign is about you—about your hopes, about your dreams, about your struggles, about securing your portion of the American Dream.[57]

NOTES

1. Barack Obama, "After Alinsky: Community Organizing in Illinois," *Illinois Issues,* University of Illinois at Springfield, 1990.
2. Christine Brozyna, "Get to Know Barack Obama," *ABC News,* November 1, 2007, http://abcnews.go.com (accessed November 21, 2007).
3. Janny Scott, "Memories of Obama in New York Differ," *New York Times,* October 29, 2007, http://www.msnbc.msn.com (accessed October 30, 2007).
4. Scott, "Memories of Obama in New York Differ."
5. Liza Mundy, "A Series of Fortunate Events," *Washington Post,* August 12, 2007, W10.

6. Ryan Lizza, "The Agitator," *New Republic,* March 19, 2007, http://www.tnr.com (accessed June 5, 2008).

7. Barack Obama, *Dreams from My Father* (New York: Three Rivers Press, 2004), 158.

8. Mundy, "A Series of Fortunate Events."

9. Ronald Roach, "Obama Rising," *Black Issues in Higher Education,* October 7, 2004, 20–23.

10. Randolph Burnside and Kami Whitehurst, "From the Statehouse to the White House? Barack Obama's Bid to Become the Next President," *Journal of Black Studies,* July 31, 2007, 75.

11. David Moberg, "Obama's Community Roots," *The Nation,* April 7, 2007, 18.

12. Larissa MacFarquhar, "The Conciliator," *The New Yorker,* May 7, 2007, http://www.newyorker.com (accessed December 18, 2007).

13. Moberg, "Obama's Community Roots," 16.

14. Ibid., 18.

15. Charles P. Pierce, "The Cynic and Senator Obama," *Esquire,* June 2008, 114.

16. Moberg, "Obama's Community Roots," 16.

17. Hank De Zutter, "What Makes Obama Run?" *Chicago Reader,* December 8, 1995, http://www.chicagoreader.com (accessed June 3, 2008).

18. Obama Says He is Emissary for Change," *Associated Press,* July 5, 2007, http://www.msnbc.msn.com (accessed July 5, 2007).

19. Michele Norris, "Michelle Obama Sees Election as Test for America," *National Public Radio,* July 9, 2007, http://www.npr.org (accessed July 9, 2007).

20. Barack Obama Web site, http://www.barackobama.com (accessed January 16, 2007).

21. Stephen Keating, "Obama Moms Cradle Campaign," *Denver Post,* June 10, 2007, C03.

22. Barack Obama, "Caucus Speech," *New York Times,* January 3, 2008, http://www.nytimes.com (accessed January 7, 2008).

23. Marc Royse, "Oprah Talks to Barack Obama," *O, the Oprah Magazine,* November 2004, 248.

24. De Zutter, "What Makes Obama Run?"

25. Steve Dougherty, *Hopes and Dreams: The Story of Barack Obama* (New York: Black Dog & Leventhal Publishers, Inc., 2007), 105.

26. Royse, "Oprah Talks to Barack Obama."

27. Ken Silverstein, "Barack Obama Inc.," *Harper's Magazine,* November 2006, 31–40.

28. Roach, "Obama Rising."

29. "Barack Obama Jumps into 2008 Race," *CBS News Online,* January 16, 2007, http://www.cbsnews.com (accessed January 16, 2007).

30. Adam Nagourney and Jeff Zeleny, "Obama Formerly Enters Presidential Race with Calls for Generational Change," *New York Times,* February 11, 2007, 22.

31. Adam Nagourney, "2 Years After Big Speech, a Lower Key for Obama," *New York Times,* April 8, 2007, 15.

32. Patrick Healy, "Courting Black Votes, Obama Emphasizes Principles," *New York Times,* April 22, 2007, 1.25.

33. MacFarquhar, "The Conciliator."

34. Patrick Healy and Michael Luo, "Edwards, Clinton and Obama Describe Journeys of Faith," *New York Times,* June 5, 2007, A20.

35. Jeff Zeleny, "The First Time Around: Senator Obama's Freshman Year," *Chicago Tribune,* December 29, 2005, http://www.chicagotribune.com/news/local/chi-051224obama,0,6232648.story (accessed May 20, 2008).

36. "The Campaign's Brightest Star," *The Economist,* June 16, 2007, 33.

37. Ron Fournier, "The Unknown: Is Obama Ready?" *Associated Press,* June 17, 2007.

38. Barack Obama, "Renewing American Leadership," *Foreign Affairs,* July/August 2007, http://www.foreignaffairs.org (accessed June 5, 2007).

39. Richard Wolffe and Daren Briscoe, "Across the Divide," *Newsweek,* July 16, 2007, 27.

40. Mundy, "A Series of Fortunate Events."

41. Ibid.

42. Ryan Lizza, "Above the Fray," *GQ,* September 2007, 408.

43. Ibid., 336.

44. Barack Obama, "A New Beginning," October 2, 2007, http://www.barackobama.com (accessed October 3, 2007).

45. Ibid.

46. Jonathan Kaufman, "Whites' Great Hope?" *Wall Street Journal,* November 10, 2007, A1.

47. Mike Littwin, "Still Waiting for Obama to Deliver Something New," *Rocky Mountain News,* November 17, 2007, 30.

48. Richard Stengel, "Interview with Barack Obama," *Time,* December 10, 2007, 40.

49. Karen Tumulty, "Obama Finds His Moment," *Time,* December 10, 2007, 45.

50. Ibid.

51. Sarah Liebowitz, "Democrats Pick Clinton," *Concord Monitor,* January 9, 2008, http://www.concordmonitor.com (accessed January 9, 2008).

52. Barack Obama, "February 12 Speech," *New York Times,* February 12, 2008, http://www.nytimes.com (accessed February 14, 2008).

53. Tom Baldwin, "Barack Obama Attacks US State of 'Racial Stalemate,' " *Times Online,* March 19, 2008, http://www.timesonline.co.uk (accessed March 19, 2008).

54. Tim Dickinson, "The Machinery of Hope," *Rolling Stone,* March 20, 2008, 38.

55. Barack Obama, "Transcript of Obama's Wesleyan Commencement Address," May 25, 2008, http://www.barackobama.com/2008/05/25/remarks_of_senator_barack_obam_70.php (accessed August 11, 2008).

56. Barack Obama, "Remarks to Indiana's Jefferson-Jackson Dinner," May 4, 2008, http://www.presidency.ucsb.edu/ws/index (accessed August 11, 2008).

57. Barack Obama, "Remarks in Raleigh, North Carolina," May 6, 2008, http://www.barackobama.com/2008/05/06/remarks_of_senator_barack_obam_62.php (accessed August 11, 2008).

CHAPTER 3

On Illinois State Politics

"There are times when I want to do everything and be everything. I want to have time to read and swim with the kids and not disappoint my voters and do a really careful job on each and every thing that I do. And that can sometimes get me into trouble. That's historically been one of my bigger faults. I mean I was trying to organize Project Vote at the same time as I was writing a book, and there are only so many hours in a day."[1]

Introduction

In 1996, Barack was elected to the Illinois state senate as a Democrat representing the Illinois 13th legislative district. During his state campaign, his platform included helping working families on Chicago's south side, an area described by *The Almanac of American Politics* as "the nation's largest urban black community for nearly a century."[2] After three years of community activism and practicing law, Barack decided to enter state politics. At the time, he said he was running because he wanted to help create jobs and a decent future for the embittered youth of the community he served. When he met with some veteran politicians to tell them of his plans, the only jobs he said they wanted to talk about were theirs and his. He also got lots of advice, some of it perplexed him, and some of it annoyed him. One suggested that he change his name, another told him to put a picture of his light-bronze, boyish face on all his campaign materials "so people don't see your name and think you're some big dark guy." Another adviser suggested that he never pose for photos with a glass in his hand—even if he wasn't drinking alcohol. Barack said,

> Now all of this may be good political advice, but it's all so superficial. I am surprised at how many elected officials—even the good ones—spend so much time talking about the mechanics of politics and not matters of substance. They have this poker chip mentality, this over-riding interest in retaining their seats or in moving their careers forward, and the business and game of politics, the political horse race, is all they talk about. Even those who are on the same page as me on the issues never seem to want to talk about them. Politics is regarded as little more than a career."[3]

Barack's arrival in Springfield in January 1997 was not met with a red carpet or open arms. Instead, many of his fellow senators cast a rather cold eye on the new senator from the south side of Chicago. Some thought he was an aloof Ivy Leaguer who spent time talking about his community organizing and his Harvard law degree. Some described Barack as an elitist and noted that many of his speeches were highly intellectual and policy-focused. When asked why he ran for the state senate, Barack answered, "Part of it was that the seat opened up. I was living in the district, and the state legislature was a part-time position. It allowed me to get my feet wet in politics and test out whether I could get something done."[4]

When Barack, a Democrat, was elected to the state senate, the state capital was in Republican control. He was known as a committed liberal and a progressive Democrat. Barack wrote that he understood state politics "as a full-contact sport, and minded neither the sharp elbows nor the occasional blind-side hit."[5]

Senator Emil Jones, Jr., who gave Barack the job of representing senate Democrats, said, "He was very aggressive when he first came to the senate. We were in the minority, but he said, 'I'd like to work hard. Any tough assignments or things you'd like me to be involved in, don't hesitate to give it to me.'"[6]

Senator Kimberly Lightford entered the state senate shortly after Barack. She recalls walking into Barack's law office and asking for advice after winning her Democratic primary. "I'm, like, very naïve and think I can fix the world—come here and change things overnight." Barack, she said, curbed her enthusiasm. Urging caution, he told her "Once you get there you might realize it's a bigger picture and you might want to look at one topic and do what you can." On her way out the door, Barack surprised her by giving her a check for her campaign. She thought, "This guy is cool. He's gorgeous. And he's giving me money! He's my new big brother."[7]

Barack's cautious, close-to-the-vest style in politics is also reflected in the way he plays poker, according to those who joined him in a regular game with lawmakers and lobbyists. Barack was "fiercely competitive, refusing to admit when he finished a night with less money than he started." Illinois State Senator Terry Link said of Barack's card playing, "He wouldn't throw money in the pot just to play out a hand. He had to know he had a darn good chance of winning."[8]

Barack persuaded Republicans to go along with initiatives, winning bipartisan support on potentially polarizing legislation: "The most important thing that you do in Springfield is you bring all sides of an issue to the table and you make them feel they are being listened to."[9]

Taking a reasonable tone and genuine attentiveness to Republican concerns in the Illinois legislature made Barack a key swing legislator for both parties, even if his voting record was decidedly liberal. "Members of both parties listened closely to him," said Kirk Dillard, Republican senator from suburban Chicago who co-sponsored legislation with Barack.[10]

Paul L. Williams, a lobbyist in Springfield, Illinois and a former state representative, said of Barack's arrival in Springfield, "He came with a huge dose of practicality," and characterized Barack's attitude as "O.K., that makes sense and sounds great, as I'd like to go to the moon, but right now I've only got enough gas to go this far."[11]

Of his time in Illinois state politics, Barack said, "I learned that if you're willing to listen to people, it's possible to bridge a lot of the differences that dominate the national political debate. I pretty quickly got to form relationships with Republicans, with individuals from rural parts of the state, and we had a lot in common."[12]

State Senator Kirk W. Dillard, a Republican, stated:

> When you come in, especially as a freshman, and work on something like ethics reform, it's not necessarily a way to endear yourself to some of the veteran members of the Illinois General Assembly. And working on issues like racial profiling was contentious, but Barack had a way both intellectually and in demeanor that defused skeptics.

Cynthia Canary, director of the Illinois Campaign for Political Reform, said of Barack, "He wasn't a maverick. There were other legislators I would turn to if I just wanted to make a lot of noise. That wasn't his style."[13]

Dan Shomon, Illinois state senate legislative aide and later Barack's Illinois campaign manager, said that when he was first asked to work with Barack in Springfield he was reluctant, having the impression that Barack could be rather testy and elitist, and that his first reaction was "I am thinking that I am really busy. He wants to change the world and that is great, but I don't really like the guy that much." After the two met, they genuinely hit it off.[14]

Shomon said, "There was a gradual progression of Barack Obama from thoughtful, earnest policy wonk/civil rights lawyer/constitutional law expert to Barack Obama the politician, the inspirer, the speaker."[15]

Denny Jacobs, a friend of Barack's and a former state senator, said,

> He stumbled on the fact that instead of running on all the issues, quote unquote, that hope is the real key. Not only the black community but less privileged people are looking for that hope. You don't have to talk about health care you have to talk about 'the promise' of

health care. Hope is a pretty inclusive word. I think he is very good at selling that.[16]

In the Illinois state senate, Barack took major risks on legislation that could have cast him as a liberal. He was the key leader behind a law requiring that all confessions and interrogations in murder cases be videotaped, a provision about which many police and prosecutors and even the Illinois' Democratic governor at first expressed doubts. "That was risky. We haven't seen that exactly on the national level," said Julie Hamos, a Democratic Illinois state representative.[17]

Like many of his colleagues, Barack played golf, pickup basketball, and made the rounds at the parties. He was also known to join the weekly poker game with legislators and lobbyists. One of his colleagues, state senator Larry Walsh, described Barack as competitive yet careful, and always hard to read. Walsh said,

> One night, we were playing … and I had a real good hand and Barack beat me out with another one. I slammed down my cards and said, "Doggone it, Barack, if you were a little more liberal in your card playing and a little more conservative in your politics, you and I would get along a lot better."[18]

Dave Syverson, a Republican committee chairman who worked on welfare reform with Barack said,

> He was passionate in his views. We had some pretty fierce arguments. We went round and round about how much to spend on day care, for example. But he was not your typical party-line politician. A lot of Democrats didn't want to have any work requirement at all for people on welfare. Barack was willing to make that deal.[19]

Mike Lawrence, director of the Public Policy Institute at Southern Illinois University, said,

> What impressed me about him was his ability in working with people of the opposite party. He had definite ideas about what ought to be contained in a campaign finance reform measure, but he also was willing to recognize that he was probably not going to get everything he wanted.[20]

John Bouman, a director of the Chicago-based National Center for Poverty Law, said,

> He is idealistic but practical. For Barack, it's not a constant flow of glorious defeats. He has good attention to ideals and core principles, but a recognition that it is good to get things done from year to year. He is willing to hammer out a good compromise, but he doesn't compromise for the sake of it.[21]

In 1999, Barack voted "present" on a vote making adult prosecution mandatory for aggravated discharge of a firearm in or near a school. He explained his vote, saying, "There is really no proof or indication that automatic transfers and increased penalties and adult penalties for juvenile offenses have, in fact, proven to be more effective in reducing juvenile crime or cutting back on recidivism."[22]

In 2000, Rich Miller, the publisher of *Capitol Fax,* a statehouse news service, said, "Barack is a very intelligent man. He hasn't had a lot of success here, and it could be because he places himself above everybody. He likes people to know he went to Harvard." Six years later, Barack met with Miller and they discussed the characterization. Miller noted,

> He took that criticism the right way and he could have taken it the wrong way. A lot of politicians, they know that they're smart. They know that they're capable. It messes with their minds. Politics is not a game of qualifications. It's a game of winning.... I just can't emphasize enough how much this guy became respected, and how transformative it was. By 2004, he just had this aura about him.[23]

In 2001, Barack voted against a measure that would have expanded the penalties for some gang activity to include the death penalty. At the time, Barack said that the bill would unfairly target minorities, stating: "There's a strong overlap between gang affiliation and young men of color.... I think it's problematic for them to be singled out as more likely to receive the death penalty for carrying out certain acts than are others who do the same thing."[24]

In June 2001, Will Marshall, an official of the moderate Democratic Leadership Council, visited Barack in Chicago. Marshall had heard good things about Barack and wanted to meet him. At the meeting, they talked about social policy after welfare reform, about the effects of globalization, and about other issues. Marshall said the following of the meeting: "I was deeply impressed. He has an analytical capacity, but he doesn't talk like a wonk—sort of like [President] Clinton."[25]

Barack ran an unsuccessful campaign against incumbent Bobby Rush for the U.S. Senate in 2000. Receiving only 31% of the vote, he returned to Springfield as someone who lost (Barack said he was "spanked" in the race), and as someone who within a short time earned the respect of his fellow senators. According to Illinois state senator Donne Trotter,

> I wouldn't say losing humbled him. Barack is a competitor, and being a competitor, you don't like to lose. When he came back, he really immersed himself in the process. He learned he had to get an agenda, to get issues he felt passionately about. He also learned some of those "get-along" qualities you need to get a bill passed. He has proven himself to me that he can take advice. He's not a one-man operation.[26]

Barack reflected on the race he lost to Representative Bobby Rush: "[T]here was very little chance of me winning that race. That was a good lesson—that you should never be too impressed with your own ideas if your name recognition in a Congressional district is only eight or whatever it was."[27] Barack wrote in his book *The Audacity of Hope*,

> Less than halfway into the campaign, I knew in my bones that I was going to lose. Each morning from that point forward I awoke with a vague sense of dread, realizing that I would have to spend the day smiling and shaking hands and pretending that everything was going according to plan.[28]

After President Clinton endorsed Rush in a radio spot, everyone knew the race was over. The race was called for Rush as Barack was set to speak to his supporters in Hyde Park, Illinois. To the crowd of about 50 supporters, he said, "I confess to you winning is better than losing."[29] Barack reflected on the loss, saying:

> I was completely mortified and humiliated, and felt terrible. The biggest problem in politics is the fear of loss. It's a very public thing, which most people don't have to go through. Obviously, the flip side

of publicity and hype is when you fall, folks are right there, snapping away. And so that is something naturally you worry about, but my hope is that I've been in this long enough and through this process enough that I take the good with the bad and don't read the good press clippings or the bad press clippings.[30]

Abner Mikva, a former federal judge and Congressman from Chicago said the following of the ill-fated campaign against Bobby Rush: "He [Barack] was very dejected when it was over and [began] thinking of how else he could use his talents."[31]

In 2004, Laimutis Nargelenas, a lobbyist for the Illinois Association of Chiefs of Police, observed that although Barack sometimes voted for "individual rights" rather than "the ability of law enforcement to get things done," he was always thoughtful on law and order and on supporting funding for police programs. Nargelenas said, "When he said he was going to do something, you could always trust him on his word."[32]

"Obama's drive to compromise goes beyond the call of political expediency—it's instinctive, almost a tic," wrote Larissa MacFarquhar of the *New Yorker* in May 2007. A friend from law school, Cassandra Butts, said,

> Barack has an incredible ability to synthesize seemingly contradictory realities and make them coherent. It comes from going from a home where white people are nurturing you, and then you go out into the world and you're seen as a black person. He had to figure out whether he was going to accept this contradiction and be just one of those things, or find a way to realize that these pieces make up the whole.

This skill served Barack well in the Illinois state senate, writes Larissa MacFarquhar. "He was unusually dexterous with opponents, and passed bills that at first were judged too liberal to have a chance."[33]

Barack said of his time in state politics:

> My experience in the state legislature is instructive. The first seven years I was there I was in the minority, and I think that I passed maybe ten bills, maybe five of them were substantive. Most of the bills that I did pass were in partnership with Republicans, because

that was the only way I could get them passed. The first year we were in the majority party I passed twenty-six bills in one year.[34]

Barack said that in Springfield he learned early

that forming relationships a lot of times was more important than having all the policy talking points in your arsenal. That most of the time people at the state level—and in the U.S. Senate—are moved as much by whether or not they trust you and whether or not they think your values are sound as they are by graphs and charts and numbers on a page.[35]

While serving in the state legislature, Barack was a senior lecturer at the University of Chicago Law School. He said,

Teaching keeps you sharp. The great thing about teaching constitutional law is that all the tough questions land in your lap: abortion, gay rights, affirmative action. And you need to be able to argue both sides. I have to be able to argue the other side as well as [conservative Supreme Court Judge Antonin] Scalia does. I think that's good for one's politics.[36]

The United Kingdom-based *The Economist* magazine said of Barack, "Mr. Obama is tough. He thrived in the world of Illinois politics, one that is dominated by entrenched political machines that pride themselves on their bare knuckle tactics."[37]

The *Chicago Tribune* endorsed Barack for his seat in the Illinois state senate and wrote the following in their editorial: "In 1996, this page endorsed a Chicago attorney, law school instructor and community activist named Barack Obama for a seat in the Illinois state senate ... our modest prediction: We said Obama 'has potential as a political leader.'" On January 27, 2008, the *Tribune* endorsed Barack for the Illinois Primary and in their editorial, reminded their readers of their 1996 endorsement and added, "He is the Democrat best suited to lead this nation. We offer him our endorsement for the February 5 Illinois Primary.... Obama can help this nation move forward.... Our takeaway: Obama has the confidence to speak truth, poll-tested or not."[38]

Barack wrote the following:

[T]hroughout my years in Springfield [Illinois], I had clung to the notion that politics could be different, and that the voters wanted something different; that they were tired of distortion, name-calling, and sound-bite solutions to complicated problems; that if I could reach those voters directly, frame the issues as I felt them, explain the choices in as truthful a fashion as I knew how, then the people's instincts for fair play and common sense would bring them around. If enough of us took that risk, I thought, not only the country's politics but the country's policies would change for the better.[39]

After losing the election to Bobby Rush, Barack was $60,000 in debt and unsure of his future. He returned to teaching and his legislative responsibilities in Springfield. He decided to try it again in the 2004 race for a U.S. Senate seat held by Republican Peter Fitzgerald and sought the assistance of Emil Jones, president of the state senate. Barack told Jones, "You've got a lot of power. You have the power to make a United State Senator." When Jones asked Barack what he had in mind, Barack described his strategy for getting elected. Jones reply was, "Let's go for it." Barack met with Marty Nesbitt, a top fundraiser, as he eyed the Senate race. Barack told Nesbitt, "If you raise $4 million, I have a 40% chance of winning. If you raise $6 million, I have a 60% chance of winning. You raise $10 million, I guarantee you I can win." Nesbitt said, "It was a matter of having the money to tell his story."[40]

While a state senator, Barack told the *New Yorker* magazine the following:

A good compromise, a good piece of legislation, is like a good sentence. Or a good piece of music. Everybody can recognize it. They say "Huh. It works. It makes sense." That doesn't happen too often [in politics], of course, but it happens.[41]

NOTES

1. David Mendell, *Obama: From Promise to Power* (New York: Amistad, 2007), 103–104.
2. Ryan Lizza, "The Natural," *Atlantic Monthly*, September 2004, 30.
3. Hank De Zutter, "What Makes Obama Run?" *Chicago Reader*, December 8, 1995, http://www.chicagoreader.com (accessed June 3, 2008).
4. Janny Scott, "In Illinois, Obama Proved Pragmatic and Shrewd," *New York Times*, July 30, 2007, http://www.nytimes.com (accessed July 30, 2007).
5. Peter Slevin, "Obama Forged Political Mettle in Illinois Capitol," *Washington Post*, February 9, 2007, A01.

6. Ibid.
7. Ron Fournier, "The Unknown: Is Obama Ready?" *Associated Press*, June 17, 2007, http://news.yahoo.com (accessed June 18, 2007).
8. Ibid.
9. Mendell, *Obama: From Promise to Power*, 128.
10. Ibid.
11. Scott, "In Illinois, Obama Proved Pragmatic and Shrewd."
12. Ibid.
13. Slevin, "Obama Forged Political Mettle in Illinois Capitol."
14. Mendell, *Obama: From Promise to Power*, 115–116.
15. Janny Scott, "In 2000, a Streetwise Veteran Schooled a Bold Young Obama," *New York Times*, September 9, 2007, 20.
16. Ibid.
17. Perry Bacon, Jr., "The Exquisite Dilemma of Being Obama," *Time*, February 20, 2006, 24.
18. Slevin, "Obama Forged Political Mettle in Illinois Capitol."
19. Joe Klein, "The Fresh Face," *Nation*, October 23, 2006, 44.
20. Slevin, "Obama Forged Political Mettle in Illinois Capitol."
21. Mendell, *Obama: From Promise to Power*, 127.
22. Sam Youngman and Aaron Blake, "Obama's Crime Votes Are Fodder for Rivals," *The Hill*, March 13, 2007, http://www.thehill.com (accessed May 12, 2008).
23. Edward McClelland, "How Obama Learned to Be a Natural," *Salon*, February 12, 2007, http://www.salon.com (accessed May 12, 2008).
24. Youngman and Blake, "Obama's Crime Votes Are Fodder for Rivals."
25. Byron York, "Obama Madness," *National Review*, November 20, 2006, 18.
26. McClelland, "How Obama Learned to Be a Natural."
27. Scott, "In 2000, a Streetwise Veteran Schooled a Bold Young Obama."
28. Ibid.
29. Michael Weisskopf, "How He Learned to Win," *Time*, May 19, 2008, 28.
30. David Remnick, "Testing the Waters," *New Yorker*, November 6, 2006, http://www.newyorker.com (accessed May 19, 2008).
31. Weisskopf, "How He Learned to Win," 28.
32. Youngman and Blake, "Obama's Crime Votes Are Fodder for Rivals."
33. Larissa MacFarquhar, "The Conciliator," *The New Yorker*, May 7, 2007, http://www.newyorker.com (accessed December 18, 2007).
34. Ken Silverstein, "Barack Obama," *Harper's Magazine*, November 2006, 31–40.
35. Scott, "In Illinois, Obama Proved Pragmatic and Shrewd."
36. Steve Dougherty, *Hopes and Dreams: The Story of Barack Obama* (New York: Black Dog & Leventhal Publishers, Inc., 2007), 78–79.
37. "Obamamania," *The Economist*, January 12, 2008, 27.
38. "For the Democrats: Obama," *Chicago Tribune*, January 27, 2008, http://www.chicagotribune.com (accessed January 28, 2008).
39. Barack Obama, *The Audacity of Hope*, (New York: Crown Publishers, 2006), 17–18.
40. Weisskopf, "How He Learned to Win," 29–30.
41. Dougherty, *Hopes and Dreams*, 85.

CHAPTER 4

On U.S. Senate Politics

"Our leaders in Washington seem incapable of working together in a practical, common-sense way. Politics has become so bitter and partisan, so gummed up by money and influence, that we can't tackle the big problems that demand solutions."[1]

"I do think there are moments in American history where there are opportunities to change the language of politics or set the country's sights in a different place, and I think we're in one of those moments."[2]

Introduction

In Barack Obama, there was always something different and exciting. For many, he represented change, a breath of fresh air, and a new possibility. It did not seem to matter to Illinois voters that Barack was a black man with an unusual heritage. Instead, they recognized he was an orator, a teacher, a legislator, and many gravitated to him. Barack wrote in his memoir *The Audacity of Hope* that his campaign for the U.S. Senate was indicative of some of the changes that have taken place in the white and black communities over the past twenty-five years. Barack wrote that Illinois already had history of blacks elected to statewide office. His race, Barack noted, did not preclude the possibility of his win, nor was his election aided by the evolving racial attitudes of Illinois' white voters. His own campaign, Barack wrote, was not a novelty.[3] It is true that although Barack entered the U.S. Senate as a celebrity, he was also recognized as one of its weakest members. He had no seniority, he was getting far more media attention than many of his experienced colleagues, and he entered a legislative body that was controlled by the other party. He also had to quickly learn the ropes. Still, he hit the ground running amid near constant questions about his possible run for the 2008 presidency.

To the ballroom packed with his supporters the night of the election for U.S. Senator, Barack said,

> I think it's fair to say that the conventional wisdom was we could not win. We didn't have enough money. We didn't have enough organization. There was no way that a skinny guy from the South Side with a funny name like Barack Obama could ever win a statewide race. Sixteen months later we are here, and Democrats from all across Illinois—suburbs, city, downstate, upstate, black, white, Hispanic, Asian—have declared: Yes, we can! Yes, we can! Yes, we can![4]

Rahm Emanuel, former Clinton aide and now a congressman from Illinois, said the following of Barack's campaigning for his U.S. Senate seat: "Twenty years ago, if I'd said there would be lawn signs with pictures of an African-American, with an African surname, all over my district on the Northwest side of Chicago, people would have had me tested for drugs. Yet there they were."[5]

Asked about his sudden stardom after winning the election in Illinois, Barack said,

The pundits and the prognosticators presumed that a skinny guy with a funny name from the South Side of Chicago couldn't get any votes outside a pretty narrow band of the electorate. I think the primary blew those assumptions out of the water. And I think people are proud of that.[6]

The chairman of the Democratic Senatorial Campaign Committee and Senator from New Jersey, John Corzine, said, "I think Barack Obama is one of the most interesting and capable individuals that is running this time, if not in any election. Frankly, he will be one of the easier candidates to raise resources for."[7]

Donna Brazile, a Democratic strategist who ran Al Gore's campaign in 2000, said of Barack, "My greatest fear for Barack is that he'll be in the background, another black face in the sea of whiteness. For now he doesn't have to become the next black leader. He has to become a great Senator from the state of Illinois."[8]

Barack said he thought the election signaled a maturing of not just black voters, but Illinois voters all across the board. He added that people in his home state showed that they were more interested in the message than the color of the messenger, adding that "I have an unusual name and an exotic background, but my values are essentially American values. I'm rooted in the African-American community, but I'm not limited by it. I think this election shows that."[9]

At a rally for Senator Russ Feingold in Milwaukee, Wisconsin in October 2004, Barack was enthusiastically introduced by Gwen Moore, a Democrat running for Congress: "He's all of us! He's not black! He's not white! He's not you know … I was going to say, he's not male, he's not female," she laughed as Barack strode onto the stage as the huge crowd cheered. Squinting in the sun, Barack surveyed the crowd and said, "My wife knows whether I'm a man or a woman. I just wanted Gwen to know that." Speaking louder to the cheering crowed, he continued to say that until recently no one knew his name, and if people knew it, they couldn't pronounce it. Then, establishing his humility, he described his vision for the Democratic Party:

There is another tradition in politics that says we're all connected. I don't just have to worry about my own child. I have to worry about the child that cannot read. It's not enough that I am part of the

African-American community. I've got to worry about the Arab-American family that John Ashcroft is rounding up, because I might be next.[10]

Barack said he was happy to have made it through his first Senate year without falling "flat on my face." In response to what makes him different, Barack answered,

> Where I probably can make a unique contribution is in helping to bring people together and bridging what I call the "empathy deficit," helping to explain the disparate factions in this country and to show them how we're joined together, helping bridge divides between black and white, rich and poor, even conservative and liberal. The story I'm interested in telling is how we can restore that sense of commitment to each other in a way that doesn't inhibit our individual responsibility, but does promote collective responsibility.[11]

During his first year in office, Barack traveled around the country raising $1.8 million for his Hopefund political action committee and devoted his public schedule to ensure Illinois voters knew he was focusing on their concerns; he held thirty-nine town meetings, most downstate where his support was not as strong as it was in Chicago. Barack noted, "If I can look back over the first year and say, 'I had a set of concrete accomplishments, even though they are not generating a lot of headlines, then I'll feel good.'"[12]

Barack arrived in Washington, D.C. after receiving 70 percent of the vote in his election, and after his speech at the Democratic National Convention. He was only the third African American elected to the Senate since Reconstruction; as a result, he was already something of a celebrity. David Axelrod, Barack's long-time friend and political advisor, said of Barack, "Very few people have come to the Senate with the kind of ballyhoo that [Obama] did, and the danger was the [he] would be viewed as a triumph of form over content. The last thing he wanted to convey was that he had 'gone Hollywood.'"[13]

Barack said of his first year as a Senator, "I think I've done a very good job meeting my responsibilities as a senator and helping the Democratic Party. I think I've done an adequate job with respect to being a husband and a father because you can always do more on those fronts."[14] When asked what was the toughest thing he had to face as a senator, Barack replied,

> Being in the minority is always tough.... I was in the state senate for seven years before I was in the U.S. Senate ... and to some degree the experiences in the state legislature are identical to Congress, except that there are a lot of reporters around in Washington and there are virtually none in the state capitol.... I went for six years, maybe passing ten bills ... and was extraordinarily frustrated. We attained the majority the seventh year and I passed twenty-six bills ... it wasn't that I was smarter in year seven than I was in year six, or more experienced; it was that we had power. And so the frustration, or the difficulty, that I feel in the U.S. Senate is very similar. You can have the best agenda in the world, but if you don't control the gavel you cannot move an agenda forward. And, when you do control the gavel, not only can you move an agenda forward but you can actually [move them]. I constantly see opportunities for collaboration across ideological lines to get stuff done. But you have to be the one who's dictating how the compromises work. If it's somebody who's not interested in compromising who's in charge, you can come up with all sorts of good ideas, and they'll stiff you. If you're the person who somebody else has to come to, you can actually engage ... and that is, by the way, the most gratifying feeling in politics, for me: when you hit that sweet spot where everybody concludes that the law that we've just passed works and is going to make things better, and everybody across party lines has to confess that we're probably better off with this thing than not.[15]

When asked how he was adjusting to Washington, D.C. and the city's political culture, Barack replied, "I have not had to partake of the culture much. My family lives in Chicago, and I'm usually here Tuesday through Thursday. I rarely meet lobbyists, it's one of the benefits of having a good staff." When asked about fundraising, he said,

> The first $250,000 that I raised was like pulling teeth. No major Democratic donors knew me, I had a funny name, they wouldn't take my phone calls. Then at a certain point we sort of clicked into the public consciousness and the buzz, and I benefited from a lot of small individual contributions that helped me get over the hump. And then after

winning, the notoriety that I received made raising money relatively simple, and so I don't have the same challenges that most candidates do now, and that's pure luck. It's one of the benefits of celebrity.[16]

When Barack was asked what he was most proud of after his first year in office, he responded, "I am really proud of the work we did on veterans affairs, because it's an issue that affects people across the state of Illinois. We were able to help close the gap in disability payments going to Illinois' disabled veterans, compared to other states."[17]

On his opposition to the Iraq war and whether he had become less vocal and why he had taken a low-key approach and had not delivered speeches on the topic when he first arrived in the Senate, Barack responded,

As a freshman, our objective was not to try to get in the front all the time. But the truth is that in that first year, we had just seen an Iraqi election, and my feeling was that while I was not optimistic, it was appropriate to try to give the nascent government a chance.[18]

In March 2006, the *National Journal* did a story on Barack and his first year in the Senate. When writer Kirk Victor asked about early impressions of the Senate, Barack responded. "I am surprised by the lack of deliberation in the World's Greatest Deliberative Body." Noting that it is a change from the state legislature, "where every bill had to be defended and subject to questions. Here, there is a lot more of competing press releases, and I think that contributes to some of the partisanship and lack of serious negotiation."[19]

Barack earned kudos from the opposite of the political aisle in his first two years in the Republican-controlled Senate. Tom Coburn, a conservative Senate Republican said,

If Barack disagrees with you or thinks you haven't done something appropriate, he's the kind of guy who'll talk to you about it. He'll come up and reconcile: "I don't think you were truthful about my bill." I've seen him do that. On the Senate floor.[20]

Coburn also said,

What Washington does is cause everybody to concentrate on where they disagree as opposed to where they agree. But leadership changes that. And Barack's got that capability, I believe—and the pizzazz and the charisma—to be a leader of America, not a leader of Democrats.[21]

Barack noted that the "blogger community" was frustrated with him because they thought he was too willing to compromise with Republicans.

My argument is that a polarized electorate plays to the advantage of those who want to dismantle government. Karl Rove can afford to win with 51 percent of the vote. They're not trying to reform health care. They are content with an electorate that is cynical about government. Progressives have a harder job. They need a big enough majority to initiate bold proposals.[22]

When asked if he was a liberal, a progressive, or a centrist, Barack answered that he likes to believe he's above all that. He says,

[T]he way I would describe myself is I think that my values are deeply rooted in the progressive tradition, the values of equal opportunity, civil rights, fighting for working families, a foreign policy that is mindful of human rights, a strong belief in civil liberties, wanting to be a good steward for the environment, a sense that the government has an important role to play, that opportunity is open to all people and that the powerful don't trample on a less powerful.[23]

Thought to have abundant political ambitions, Barack was seen as taking a cautious and nonconfrontational approach to his policymaking.

Since the founding, the American political tradition has been reformist, not revolutionary. What that means is that for a political leader to get things done, he or she ideally should be ahead of the curve, but not too far ahead. I want to push the envelope but make sure I have enough folks with me that I'm not rendered politically impotent.[24]

Despite concerns over Barack's level of experience and his short time in the U.S. Senate, Eric Zorn, columnist for the *Chicago Tribune,* wrote the following:

Obama has served in the minority party in the U.S. Senate for two years—not a position with much leverage. Still, he managed to get his name on sunshine legislation to track and search government spending online, action to send additional humanitarian relief to the Congo and a nuclear threat reduction program. He's also promoted the interests of military veterans."[25]

Gregory Craig, an attorney with Williams & Connolly and a longtime Democratic figure, said of Barack, "I liked his sense of humor and the confidence he had discussing national issues, especially as a state senator. You felt excited to be in his presence." He added that Barack is not seen as a "polarizer" like other African American leaders such as Jesse Jackson and Al Sharpton, adding, "He gets respect from his adversaries because of the way he treats them. He doesn't try to be all things to all people, but he has a way of taking positions you don't like without making you angry."[26]

Democratic presidential nominee Senator Barack Obama smiles as he is introduced at a state Democratic election celebration party in Manchester, New Hampshire, December 10, 2006. (AP Photo/Jim Cole)

While Obama has drawn praise from Democrats and Republicans for his intellect and diligence, he's struggling to please all those who expect something from him: liberals want the formerly feisty antiwar candidate to be the standard bearer for their causes, Democrats in Washington want him to take on Bush, African-Americans want the only black Senator to speak out on racial issues, and moderates and Republicans like McCain want to see Obama's bipartisan side. It's a complicated balance, particularly for a man who would need the support of all those disparate groups to become President.[27]

David Axelrod said, "People have enormous expectations of him. And to live up to them is difficult. He's just a person, and the minute you start casting votes, you make some people happy and some people unhappy."[28] Barack said,

You should always assume that when I cast a vote or make a statement it is because it is what I believe in. The thing that bothers me is the assumption that if I make a judgment that's different from yours, then it must mean I am less progressive or my goals are different, meaning I must be not really committed to helping people.[29]

Congressman Bobby Rush, of Illinois, said: "I think that Obama, his election to the Senate, was divinely ordered. I'm a preacher and a pastor; I know that that was God's plan. Obama has certain qualities that—I think he is being used for some purpose."[30]

Senator John McCain said of Barack: "He is a voice of strength and moderation, an American success story."[31]

NOTES

1. Steve Dougherty, *Hopes and Dreams: The Story of Barack Obama* (New York: Black Dog & Leventhal Publishers, Inc., 2007), 113.

2. Ibid., 99.

3. Barack Obama, *The Audacity of Hope* (New York: Crown Publishers, 2006), 234, 240.

4. Monica Davey, "As Quickly as Overnight, a Democratic Star Is Born," *New York Times,* March, 18, 2004, A.20.

5. Dougherty, *Hopes and Dreams*, 89.

6. Ryan Lizza, "The Natural," *Atlantic Monthly,* September 2004, 30–33.

7. Davey, "As Quickly as Overnight, a Democratic Star Is Born."

8. Amanda Ripley, David Thigpen, and Jeannie McCabe, "Obama's Ascent," *Time,* November 15, 2004, 74–81.

9. Davey, "As Quickly as Overnight, a Democratic Star Is Born."

10. Ripley, Thigpen, and McCabe, "Obama's Ascent."

11. Jodi Enda, "Great Expectations," *American Prospect,* February 5, 2006.

12. Jeff Zeleny, "The First Time Around: Senator Obama's Freshman Year," *Chicago Tribune,* December 29, 2005, http://www.chicagotribune.com/news/local/chi-051224obama,0,6232648.story (accessed May 20, 2008).

13. Kirk Victor, "Reason to Smile," *National Journal,* March 18, 2006, 18–27.

14. Zeleny, "The First Time Around."

15. David Remnick, "Testing the Waters," *The New Yorker,* November 6, 2006, http://www.newyorker.com (accessed May 18, 2008).

16. Ken Silverstein, "Barack Obama Inc.," *Harper's Magazine,* November 2006, 31–40.

17. Kirk Victor, "In His Own Words: Barack Obama," *National Journal,* March 18, 2006, 22–23.

18. Jeff Zeleny, "As Candidate, Obama Carves Antiwar Stance," *New York Times,* February 26, 2007, http://www.nytimes.com (accessed February 26, 2007).

19. Victor, "Reason to Smile."

20. Dougherty, *Hopes and Dreams*, 105–106.

21. Ibid.

22. Silverstein, "Barack Obama Inc."

23. Enda, "Great Expectations."

24. Silverstein, "Barack Obama Inc."

25. Eric Zorn, "Obama Critics Build Cases on Faulty Premises," *Chicago Tribune,* December 19, 2006. Quoted in John K. Wilson, *Barack Obama, This Improbable Quest* (Boulder, CO: Paradigm Publishers, 2008), 153.

26. Silverstein, "Barack Obama Inc."

27. Perry Bacon, Jr., "The Exquisite Dilemma of Being Obama," *Time,* February 20, 2006, 24.

28. Ibid.

29. David Sirota, "Mr. Obama Goes to Washington," *The Nation,* June 8, 2006, http://www.thenation.com (accessed May 19, 2008).

30. Janny Scott, "In 2000, a Streetwise Veteran Schooled a Bold Young Obama," *New York Times,* September 9, 2007, 20.

31. Dougherty, *Hopes and Dreams*, 46.

CHAPTER 5

On the Campaign for the Presidency and the Concerns and Criticisms of His Campaign

"I'm not somebody who at the age of 5 or 6 dreamed about being president. It's not something that I'm focused on right now, but it's not something that I would foreclose in the future."[1]

"Are you thinking about Obama '08? It is not going to happen. I don't intend to run for president in the next election."[2]

"I'm in this to win, I want to win, and I think we will win. But I'm also going to emerge intact. I'm going to be Barack Obama and not some parody."[3]

Introduction

On July 27, 2004, Illinois state senator Barack Obama delivered the keynote speech at the Democratic National Convention. He said, "Tonight is a particular honor for me because, let's face it, my presence on this stage is pretty unlikely." As he spoke, the audience listened with rapt attention. When he finished his speech, they excitedly waved their arms, hats, and signs, and were obviously thrilled with what they had just heard. Those watching on television said that they had cheered, some said they stood up and clapped, and some even admitted they danced. For days, people wondered what had happened and who this man was. For many Democrats, the speech was electrifying and inspiring; for Democrats, it was a joyful time. Those from the other side of the political aisle who watched and listened had to agree that this fresh face, this politico, unknown to nearly everyone in the country outside of his home state of Illinois, had just delivered a remarkable speech. Many wanted to know more about him and where he came from. They asked why was he selected to deliver such an important speech at the Democratic National Convention at a time described by many as a very contentious one in American politics. When Barack delivered the speech, he was in the midst of a campaign for the U.S. Senate. In November, he won the contest by a landslide, and in January 2005 he was sworn in as the only African American currently in the Senate. At the time, Barack was not a household name and few knew him outside of the state of Illinois. But it was not long before there were whispers and then louder voices about the junior senator from Illinois running for president. In February 2007, Barack announced his candidacy. He had already been testing the waters by visiting the early primary and caucus states. He formally announced his candidacy in Springfield in front of the Old State Capitol Building, and in front of thousands of supporters standing in the frigid cold air of an Illinois winter.

As Obama campaigned for the presidency, he stumbled as most politicians have and still do. In his speeches and in his statements to huge crowds, to audiences in small venues, and to the ever-present gaggle of media that constantly surrounds him, Barack has said things that have been misconstrued and taken out of context. He has, like most people in the public eye, made mistakes and made decisions based on political advantage, such as deciding not to accept public financing. Those who supported him and spoke on his behalf have also stumbled, and his opponents are quick to criticize and use his gaffes and errors in their own campaigning. The twenty-four-hour news cycle also has continually used his errors, and the errors made by other candidates, sometimes running a constant loop of video. There are the pundits who talk incessantly about what was said, how it was said, or what was not said or done.

Throughout the long campaign, there have also been concerns and criticisms voiced about Barack's experience and/or the lack thereof; there have been questions about his faith, and whether he was all talk and no specifics. For a time, the missteps, the misspoken words, and the mistakes seemed to be never ending. From his former pastor's fiery rhetoric, which forced Barack eventually to leave his church, to the rumors of being a Muslim, to being endorsed by terrorists, to being criticized for not wearing a flag pin, and to questions about his patriotism, Barack has had his critics and skeptics. Yet he seems to never lose his cool and has generally kept his message and campaign on track. It has been a campaign that has been more than a year in the making, and like all politicians, Obama has found that he has had to explain himself, deflect the criticisms, and address the concerns. Most observe that he has an amazing talent to fire up a crowd, that his ability to draw thousands of people throughout the campaign has not been seen before, and that his speaking and rhetorical skills are unmatched; but his debate skills, others have observed, need to be polished, and his message needs more specifics. There have been many debates with his rivals, and as the field narrowed to one competitor, Senator Hillary Clinton from New York, there were more debates. It has been a long and arduous battle, and the primary season continued until June 4, 2008, when Barack became the presumptive nominee for the Democratic Party to face Senator John McCain from Arizona, the Republican presumptive nominee, in the general election in November 2008.

The Campaign for the Presidency

Politics didn't lead me to working folks. Working folks led me to politics.[4]

David Axelrod said, "The first conversation about the presidential campaign was that there was not going to be a presidential campaign." Barack agreed and added,

> We very deliberately tried to tamp down expectations. I didn't do any national interviews until Katrina. I tried to be very deliberate in terms of the work that I did here in the U.S. Senate. I didn't file a lot of symbolic bills—like a universal health care bill or other legislation that I wasn't in a position to pass because we were in a minority party.[5]

In the fall of 2006, as Barack was on a book tour to promote his second book, *The Audacity of Hope*, his friends encouraged him to be open about his presidential ruminations. The result was a wave of national publicity. *Time* put him on the cover with the headline, "Why Barack Obama Could Be the Next President."[6] On October 22, 2006, Barack appeared on the NBC television show *Meet the Press* with commentator Tim Russert. In an attempt to get a straight answer about whether he would run, Russert's interview went as follows:

Russert: But it's fair to say you're thinking about running for president in 2008?

Barack: It's fair, yes.

Russert: And so when you said to me in January [2006], "I will not." That statement is no longer operative.

Barack: The—I would say that I am still at the point where I have not made a decision to, to pursue higher office, but it is true that I have thought about it over the last several months.

Russert: So, it sounds as if the door has opened a bit.

Barack: A bit.[7]

In November 2006, Barack and Michelle met with a team of advisors to discuss a possible campaign for the presidency. Michelle said, "I want you to show me how you're going to do this. You need to show me that this is not going to be a bullshit fly-by-night campaign." A month later, there was another meeting with advisors, and soon the word was out that Barack was considering a run.[8]

In late 2006, Barack had dinner with some of the Democrats' most powerful African American women. Several had already committed their support to Senator Hillary Clinton. Of the dinner meeting, Barack said,

> A lot of those women are good friends; they'd all be supporters of mine if I just stayed in the U.S. Senate. Talking with them about potentially running for president caused some conflicts, because a sizeable number of them are very close to Senator Clinton. I think there's no doubt that it would be easier for a lot of people in Washington if I had decided that I was going to take a pass and wait my appropriate turn, which might be, from their perspective, 10 years from now, or at least once the Clintons had exhausted all possibilities of running any further.[9]

Michelle said of her husband's possible run for the presidency: "I took myself down every dark road you could go on, just to prepare myself before we jumped out there." She wondered if they were really emotionally and financially ready and that she had dreamed out all the scenarios she could think of. She concluded that the bottom line was that the little sacrifice they had to make was nothing compared to the possibility of what they could do if his campaign caught on.[10]

In November 2006, the *Washingtonian* magazine featured an article entitled, "The Legend of Barack Obama." At the same time, a Google search noted such adjectives as "superstar" and "rock star" and "electrifying." And it was not just Democrats who were excited; a Republican operative was quoted as referring to Barack as a "walking, talking hope machine."[11]

Democrats and Republicans alike saw Barack as a formidable candidate. A former fellow Illinois senator said, "In Republican circles, we've always feared that Barack would become a rock star of American politics."[12]

According to a Democratic Party strategist in November 2006, Barack had yet to be tested or scrutinized and the Republicans had yet to pore over his past. Barack would, the strategist determined, be a stronger candidate if he had been through the fire and had more experience, noting "If he had gone from state senator to governor, and he had served one term as governor and was running for president, it would be a much more compelling case (for running in 2008). Then he would have been in a situation in which he was a final decision-maker."[13]

On a frigid day in February 2007, in front of the Old State Capitol building in Springfield, Illinois and an estimated 10,000 people, Barack Obama told America, and indeed the world, that he was running for president of the United States. With Michelle at his side, and his two young daughters trailing right behind, a confident Barack walked to the podium and gazed out at a crowd filled with supporters and the media, all anxiously waiting to listen. Wearing an overcoat to ward off the stiff wind and single-digit temperatures, the gloveless Barack presented himself as an agent for generational change and as someone who intended to transform a government in shambles from cynicism, corruption, and a "smallness of our politics." He told the crowd, "The time for that politics is over. It is through. It's time to turn the page." Portraying his candidacy as a movement rather than a campaign, he said, "Each and every time, a new generation has risen up and done what's needed to be done. Today we are called once more, and it is time for our generation to answer that call."[14]

He assured the crowd and the country that he was not interested in politics as usual, stating, "I recognize there is a certain presumptuousness in this—a certain audacity—to this announcement. I know that I haven't spent a lot of time learning the ways of Washington. But I've been there long enough to know that the ways of Washington must change." Barack told the crowd that he knew his appeal would only take him so far and that his campaign was built from the ground up and that it would build and grow and give his supporters a sense of ownership in seeking a change in America. As a grassroots political outsider, he said his campaign cannot only be about him, it must be about the people and about what he and the American people can do together, and that together, he added, they could transform a nation.[15]

Barack's decision to run for president would be no surprise to the citizens who lived in western Kenya, Barack's ancestral home. They knew their favorite son was destined for great things. Barack's step-grandmother, in her mid-80s, who encouraged his father to study in the United States said, "I have had a dream you see, a recurring dream.... I have seen Barack surrounded by soldiers in dress uniform. At first I did not understand it, but now I realize it is because he is president." His step-grandmother added that when she first met Barack on his first visit to Kenya, she knew he was special and "praised God" that he had been able to have such a good education.

Here we all believe education is the key ... his father had always talked about how well he was doing at school. When he came to stay with us the first time it must have been difficult, but he never let it show. He ate the same food as the rest of us, eggs, goat, sometimes fish.[16]

From the onset, Barack pledged to run "a different kind of campaign," one without mudslinging and personal attacks. He said,

> The campaigns shouldn't be about making each other look bad. They should be about figuring out how we can all do some good for this precious country of ours. That's our mission. And in this mission, our rivals won't be one another, and I would assert it won't even be the other party. It's going to be cynicism that we're fighting against.[17]

Barack was explicit from the beginning: there was to be "no drama." He told his aides, "I don't want elbowing or finger-pointing. We're going to rise or fall together." He wanted steady, calm, focused leadership; he wanted to keep out the grandstanders and make sure the quiet dissenters spoke up.[18] Barack said,

> The one thing I am absolutely certain of, is that if all I'm offering is the same Democratic narrative that has been offered for the last 20 years, then there's really no point in my running, because Senator Clinton is going to be very adept at delivering that message. What makes it worthwhile for me to run is the belief that we can actually change the narrative and create a working majority that we haven't seen in a very long time—and that, frankly, the Clintons never put together.[19]

> I don't want to spend the next year, or the next four years, refighting the same fights we had in the 1990s. I don't want to pit red America against blue America. I want to be president of the United States of America.[20]

The Economist magazine said in December 2007,

> Mr. Obama is recapturing the excitement that made his campaign such a spectacle of cheering crowds and kerchinging coffers.... And Mr. Obama is beginning to offer something that has eluded him so far—the sense that he just might win ... [he] is probably the best placed candidate to turn a good Democratic year into a landslide ... but he still has to prove he is made of presidential stuff.[21]

By the end of March 2007, Barack announced his campaign had raised more than 100,000 donations totaling at least $25 million, including $6.9 million generated through Internet donations. A great percentage of the donors were first-time donors who sent $50 to $100 checks from home computers. Barack's campaign finance chair, Penny Pritzker, stated, "This overwhelming response, in only a few short weeks, shows the hunger for a different kind of politics in this country and a belief at the grassroots level that Barack Obama can bring out the best in America to solve our problems."[22]

Barack said,

> If you're involved in any profession, I think your goal is to be at the top of your profession and to do your best. I wouldn't be involved in politics if I didn't want to influence the debate significantly. And obviously the president has more influence than anyone over the direction of our country.[23]

On the cusp of an historic decision over whether to run for the White House, Barack said he believed he could move the nation beyond the generational politics that have defined the last forty years.

> Do I have something that is sufficiently unique to offer to the country that is worth putting my family through a presidential campaign? Politically, I think I would be a viable candidate. So that's a threshold question and I wouldn't run if I didn't think I could win....

Speaking to the experience of Vice President Dick Cheney, a former defense secretary, and Defense Secretary Donald Rumsfeld, Barack added that they "had the best resume on paper of any foreign policy team and the result has been what I consider to be one of the biggest foreign policy mistakes in our history."[24]

Columnist Peggy Noonan, writing for the *Wall Street Journal*, noted the following in December 2006:

> We are getting very excited. Barack Obama is brilliant, eloquent and fresh. He is "exciting" (David Brooks), "charming" (Bob Schieffer), "my favorite guy" (Oprah Winfrey), has "charisma" (Donna Brazile), and should run now for president (George Will). Our political and

media establishments, on the rebound from bad history, are sounding like Marlene Dietrich in her little top hat. *Falling in luff again, vot am I to do, vot am I to do?*[25]

Barack said he understood that people no longer had confidence in their elected leaders and that they believed "government feels like a business instead of a mission." His campaign, he told a crowd of about 1,500 supporters in Denver "was their campaign," and that "the country calls us." He added, "We have to take over Washington. At every juncture when the people decided to change this country, it changed." Michael J. Williams, a Denver chef, stood near the front of the stage as Barack spoke at the rally. He said he already knew he was backing Barack as president, stating, "He has soul and a conscience, and he's looking out for Joe Blow."[26]

Newton Minow, a Chicago lawyer who served in the Kennedy administration said, "This is the sort of thing you get once in a generation. This is a connection between what the voters need and what the voters want. This is the first time I've felt it since Jack Kennedy."[27]

Barack's ambition sometimes makes him overly cautious and he rarely plays the attack dog for his party. A Senate Democratic aide said, "He's very carefully chosen what assignments he will take." Some Democrats complained about his high-profile alliances with Republicans, such as him joining with Tom Coburn, one of the most conservative Republicans in the Senate, to push a bill to monitor Hurricane Katrina recovery spending. "He needs to be careful not to look too political and too out for himself. He needs to pick some fights [with Republicans]," said a Democratic strategist in February 2006.[28]

The global interest in the 2008 presidential race and particularly in Barack triggered intense media coverage oversees. Barack played well in Tokyo, London, Frankfurt, and Nairobi. In late February 2007, one of Japan's top networks broadcast a special on Barack that sent its ratings soaring. Washington bureau chief Tadayoshi Li said, "Historically, they've known Hillary Clinton a long time. Now, Obama has become the first and only candidate to equal Clinton's star power in Tokyo. Other candidates, not so much." Marco Bardazzi, a Washington-based correspondent for the ANSA Italian News Agency, which serves audiences in Latin America in addition to Italy, has covered two presidential campaigns. He said, "Hillary and Barack are the big stars as far as the coverage is concerned. For us to have Italian journalists traveling to Springfield, Illinois, two years before the election is, by Italian standards, crazy." The British press showed similar interests in Barack, sending one of their correspondents to Springfield for Barack's announcement to run for president. "The fact is, because of this country's importance and all its recent screw-ups, the politics of the succession of George W. Bush are watched like a hawk. I get the sense British readers are more interested in American politics than British politics."[29]

David Sirota, a Democratic activist said, "He's got all the talent. The question is, are you willing to be criticized, willing to be attacked?"[30]

When asked what constitutes being ready for the office of the presidency, Barack answered,

> I don't know exactly what makes somebody ready to be President. It's not clear that J.F.K. was "ready" to be President, it's not clear that Harry Truman, when he was elevated, was "ready," and yet, somehow, some people respond and some people don't. My instinct is that people who are ready are folks who go into it understanding the gravity of their work, and are able to combine vision and judgment. Having knowledge is important. I'm one of those folks—I wouldn't probably fit in with the Administration—who actually thinks that being informed is a good basis for policy ... when you are in Washington, what struck me was how many really smart, capable people are around you all the time, offering you great ideas on every problem under the sun.[31]

Laurence Tribe, a liberal scholar at Harvard Law School who once employed Barack as a research assistant, said,

> He brings to politics a desire to find common ground, which makes it impossible to predict exactly how he would line up on various people's litmus test issues. I think he comes at things in a way that is perpendicular to the usual left-right axis.[32]

Barack said,

> You know, I think we're in a moment of history where probably the most important thing we need to do is to bring the country together, and one of the skills that I bring to bear is being able to pull together

the different strands of American life and ... focus on what we have in common ... I know that I haven't spent a lot of time learning the ways of Washington. But I've been there long enough to know the ways of Washington must change.... It's possible that, you know, after we go through this whole process that the voters conclude: "You know what. He's not ready." And I respect that. I don't expect that simply because I can move people in speeches that that automatically qualifies me for this job. I think that I have to be tested and run through the paces, and I have to earn this job.[33]

David Axelrod said,

Obama's history is that he's been progressive and pragmatic and been able to work with both sides of the aisle and people across the ideological spectrum to get things done. He comes to the tale with a point of view, but he's not dogmatic or rigid. He's willing to compromise on details without sacrificing his principles.[34]

When Barack took his campaign to Wisconsin for the February 19, 2008 primary, he told an estimated crowd of 17,000 cheering supporters,

"Tonight we are on our way. We also know at this moment the cynics can no longer say that our hope is false. We have now won east and west, north and south, and across the heartland of this country we love. We have given young people a reason to believe, and brought folks back to the polls who want to believe again. And we are bringing together Democrats and Independents and Republicans; blacks and whites; Latinos and Asians; small states and big states, and Red States and Blue States, into the United States of America.[35]

If the election was one where a candidate wins by virtue of being seen as winning, the definition of momentum, it would mean that voters in future primary and caucus contests would be influenced by the outcome of all the earlier contests.[36]

"It's not experience that people are demanding. It's capability. It's not 'have you done it before?' It's 'could you do it in the future?' And Obama has that 'could-do-it' image," said Republican pollster Frank Luntz in the *National Journal*.[37]

Tony Bullock, a former Hill staffer and vice president at Ogilvy Public Relations Worldwide, said of Barack, "It's not as though he's the accidental senator, but, to some degree, his political story is a series of random walks and chance encounters."[38]

"I like to believe that we can have a leader whose family name is not Bush or Clinton. I like what Obama had to say," said a fifty-three-year-old retired software engineer after hearing Barack speak in New Hampshire.[39]

A sixty-three-year-old man at a Denver rally said, "He gives me hope as a presidential candidate. He will win because the American public is ready for a change. He's energized people to a level I haven't seen since JFK and RFK."[40]

Will Marshall, an official of the Democratic Leadership Council stated, "Is four years [in the Senate] enough? It may be too many. Long service in the Senate doesn't necessarily prepare you well for the rigors of a presidential campaign and for crafting a broad message."[41]

Barack's race was often discussed; his deemed inexperience to be president was also a matter of discussion. One comparison was to John F. Kennedy. Theodore Sorensen, JFK's speechwriter and political advisor, said,

> He [Obama] reminds me in many ways of Kennedy in 1960. The pundits said he was Catholic and too young and inexperienced and wasn't a member of the party's inner circle. They forgot that the nomination wasn't decided in Washington but out in the field.[42]

He was also compared to another former president, Bill Clinton, in style, a natural ease with people, and an ability to win people over. Like Clinton, Barack presented himself as "a new kind of politician who can rise above and bridge partisan differences."[43]

"Obamamania" was rampant throughout the country, and the political and societal forces clamoring for new ideas, a new face, and politics of hope offering a less bitter brand of politics were gathering speed. In January 2007, Barack told *U.S. News & World Report*,

> I think there is a great hunger for change in the country—and not just policy change. What I also think they are looking for is change in tone and a return to some notion of the common good and some sense of cooperation, of pragmatism over ideology. I'm a stand-in for that right now.[44]

Republican pollster Frank Luntz said of Barack in January 2007,

> Everyone can see themselves in Obama. He is the definition of the American dream, the definition of the American promise.... Conservatives see him as clean-cut and businesslike, while moderates see him as a problem solver. Liberals see him as a man from a multicultural background who breaks down racial and other barriers.[45]

Andrew Sullivan, in his article that appeared in the December 2007 edition of *The Atlantic*, wrote, "Obama is the only candidate who can take America—finally—past the debilitating, self-perpetuating family quarrel of the Baby Boom generation." Barack said, "When I think of Baby Boomers, I think of my mother's generation. And I was too young for the formative period of the '60s—civil rights, sexual revolution, Vietnam War. Those all sort of passed me by."[46]

> I think that there's the possibility—not the certainty, but the possibility—that I can't just win an election but can also transform the country in the process, that the language and the approach I take to politics is sufficiently different that I could bring diverse parts of this country together in a way that hasn't been done in some time, and that bridging those divisions is a critical element in solving problems like health care or energy or education.[47]

Writer Larissa MacFarquhar, wrote in *The New Yorker*, "He has staked his candidacy on union—on bringing together two halves of America that are profoundly divided, and by associating himself with Lincoln—and he knows what both of those things mean."[48]

Barack was in a feisty, even peevish mood one day when he pushed back against the idea that he was all style and no substance. He told the reporters,

> The fact of the matter is, I have *the* most specific plan in terms of how to get out of Iraq of any candidate. I have delivered speeches over the course of the two years, before I started running for president, on every major issue out there, whether it's education, health care, or energy. I've written two books that have sold close to a million copies each that probably give people more insight into how I think and how I feel about the issues facing America than any

candidate who's run for office in recent memory. The problem is not that the information is not out there. The problem is that that's not what you guys have been reporting on. You've been reporting on how I look in a swimsuit.[49]

Oprah Winfrey said the following:

Experience in the hallways of government isn't as important to me as experience on the pathway of life. I challenge you to see through those people who try and convince you that experience with politics as usual is more valuable than wisdom won from years of service people outside the walls of Washington, D.C. ... What we need is, we need a new way of doing business in Washington, D.C. and in the world. You know, I am so tired. I'm tired of politics as usual. That's why you seldom see politicians on my show—because I only have an hour.... We the people can see through all that rhetoric. We recognize that the amount of time that you've spent in Washington means nothing unless you're accountable for the judgments you made with the time you had. We need good judgment. We need Barack Obama.[50]

Oprah Winfrey has also said,

[F]or the very first time in my life I feel compelled to stand up and speak out for the man who I believe has a new vision for America. Over the years, I have voted for as many Republicans as I have Democrats. This isn't about partisanship for me. This is very, very personal. I'm here because of my personal conviction about Barack Obama and what I know he can do for America.[51]

Barack said the following after his victory in the Iowa Caucus:

They said this day would never come. They said our sights were set too high. They said this country was too divided, too disillusioned. But on this January night, at this defining moment in history, you have done what the cynics said we couldn't do. We are one nation. We are one people and our time for change has come. In New Hampshire, if you give me the same chance that Iowa did tonight, then I will be that president for America.[52]

An Iowa Caucus voter said on January 4, 2008, "Obama has tremendous passion. I think a lot of Democrats are desperate for that."[53] The day after the Iowa Caucus victory, David Brooks, columnist for the *New York Times*, wrote, "Americans are going to feel good about the Obama victory, which is a story of youth, possibility and unity through diversity.... Obama has achieved something remarkable.... Obama is changing the tone of American liberalism, and maybe American politics, too."[54] After the Iowa Caucus and New Hampshire Primary, the *Economist* said,

> Mr. Obama has demonstrated a unique ability to invoke passion among his supporters. This is partly because at his best he may be the finest public speaker of his generation: a man who echoes John Kennedy and Martha Luther King but nevertheless speaks in a voice that is all his own. It is not just that he says it well: it is also what he says.[55]

After Barack lost the New Hampshire Primary, he conceded the race to Senator Clinton and in his speech he had a new slogan: "Yes we can!" He told his supporters the following:

> A few weeks ago, no one imagined that we'd have accomplished what we did here tonight. For most of this campaign, we were far behind, and we always knew our climb would be steep. But in record numbers, you came out and spoke up for change ... there is something happening in America ... when Americans who are young in age and in spirit—who have never before participated in politics—turn out in numbers we've never seen because they know in their hearts that this time must be different ... when people vote not just for the party they belong to but the hopes they hold in common. All of the candidates in this race share these goals. All have good ideas. And all are patriots who serve this country honorably. But the reason our campaign has always been different is because it's not just about what I will do as President, it's also about what you, the people who love this country, can do to change it. That's why tonight belongs to you. It belongs to the organizers and the volunteers and the staff who believed in our improbable journey and rallied so many others to join. But in the unlikely story that is America, there has never been anything false about hope.... Yes we can ... yes we can to justice and

equality. Yes we can to opportunity and prosperity. Yes we can heal this nation. Yes we can repair this world. Yes we can.[56]

Massachusetts Senator Edward Kennedy endorsed Barack in February 2008. He said,

There's no question that he has tapped into something. I don't think there's any question that it's a phenomenon and it is broadening. But I'm mindful that crowds don't always turn into votes. These campaigns go through different transitions. He has a very engaging kind of charm, and that is going to become stronger and stronger as he gets known.[57]

On February 9, 2008, the United Kingdom-based *The Economist* magazine noted, "Mr. Obama is the most inspiring American politician for a generation.... Mr. Obama's supporters want a president who can inspire Americans to be their better selves."[58]

In 1980, so called Reagan Democrats played a key role in electing a new president. In 2007, Obama Republicans seemed to be emerging as a significant political force, at least in the early primaries. One Republican, a twenty-eight-year-old who voted for Bush twice, said, "I'm a conservative but I have gay friends.... I don't feel like Obama is condemning me for being a Republican." A former marine and self-described lifelong Republican said, "The Republican Party has become so ugly and so arrogant, I don't want to have any part of it." Barack talked about his Republican supporters, saying "They whisper to me. They say, 'Barack, I'm a Republican, but I support you.' And I say, 'Thank you. Why are we whispering?'"[59]

In an interview with *Newsweek* magazine in February 2008, Barack was asked, "Isn't it accurate for a fair-minded observer to say Hillary would be more ready on day one?" Barack responded,

No. The question isn't who's ready on day one, but who's right on day one. A mythology has been created that somehow just by being there for eight years [in the White House as First Lady], she is going to be better prepared, better organized and exercise better judgment. But I would put my judgments on foreign policy next to hers over the last four years on Iraq, on Iran, on how would she conduct diplomacy, on Pakistan. I would argue that reflects readiness, not the fact that you sat in the White House or that you traveled to 82 countries.[60]

Speaking about his opponent, Senator Hillary Clinton, Barack said,

She's made the argument that she's thoroughly vetted, in contrast to me. I think it's important to examine that argument because if the suggestion is somehow that on issues of ethics or disclosure or transparency that she's going to have a better record than I have and will be better able to withstand Republican attacks, I think that's an issue that should be tested.

Barack responded to Senator Clinton's claim she is better prepared to protect the nation and her touting of her experience on foreign policy with the following:

It's important to examine that claim and not just allow her to assert it, which I think has been going on for quite some time. What exactly is this foreign experience that she's claiming? I know she talks about visiting 80 countries. It is not clear, was she negotiating treaties or agreements, or was she handling crises during this period of time? My sense is the answer's no. I have not seen any evidence that she is better equipped to handle a crisis. If the only criteria is longevity in Washington, then she's certainly not going to compete with John McCain on that.[61]

On the question of a "Dream Ticket" with Barack as the vice president and Senator Hillary Clinton as the president, Barack said the following:

With all respect, I won twice as many states as Senator Clinton. I won more of the popular vote than Senator Clinton. I won more delegates than Senator Clinton. So I do not know how someone who is in second place is offering the vice presidency to someone who is in first place ... [and] how it is if I'm not ready, how you think I can be such a great vice-president.... I am not running for vice-president, I'm running for President of the United States of America. I'm running to be commander-in-chief. The reason I'm running to be commander-in-chief is because I believe that the most important thing when you answer that phone call at 3:00 AM is what kind of judgment you have.[62]

Suggesting Barack should become his wife's running mate, President Bill Clinton said,

I know that she has always been open to it, because she believes that if you can unite the energy and the new people that he's brought in and the people in these vast swathes of small-town and rural America that she's carried overwhelmingly, if you had those two things together she thinks it'd be hard to beat.[63]

An Ohio supporter said on March 12, 2008,

I'm praying that he wins, I really am. This country is ready for change, but it's not just him. The president can only do so much. He's got to surround himself with qualified people, and the citizens have to work, too.[64]

At first stating that he would remain neutral in the campaign, Senator Bob Casey of Pennsylvania later endorsed Barack in March 2008, in part to broker reconciliation between Barack and Hillary Clinton. He said,

I believe in my heart that there is one person who's uniquely qualified to lead us in that new direction and that is Barack Obama. I really believe that in a time of danger around the world and in division here at home, Barack Obama can lead us, he can heal us, he can help rebuild America … for a long time, I was not only neutral, I was undecided, an undecided voter. I know a lot about campaigns and a lot about our state, I think it's very important that I make the decision public. A campaign can test someone; he's been tested. He's appealed to the better angels of our nature under very difficult circumstances.[65]

Margaret Campbell, a Montana state legislator, declared her support of Barack in April 2008. She said, "Senator Obama reminds me of why I'm a Democrat. I think he can win a general election. He gives me that belief that America can be united.[66]

As Barack's supporters continued to drum up support, they said they were hearing the persistent rumor that Barack was a Muslim and questions about his patriotism. Barack responded,

> It frustrates me that people would even have a question about something like that, because they don't ask the same questions of some of the other candidates. If they don't vote for me, it should be because they think Senator Clinton or Senator McCain have better ideas. It shouldn't be because they think I am less patriotic or because they question what my religious faith is.[67]

In May 2008, prior to the Indiana Primary, Barack changed tactics. Instead of speaking at large rallies and arenas, he moved around the state, speaking at diners, retirement homes, and to smaller groups. "What I want to do is spend more time listening than talking. It's been wonderful to see these big crowds, but the problem is you don't really learn much when you're listening to yourself talk." At such a gathering, Barack responded to a question: "You want to know my values? Let me tell you about my family." Barack responded to continuing questions about who he really is with the following:

> Because we've been so successful, that's why my opponents have been trying to make this election about me lately. "We're not sure he shares our values. We haven't seen him wear a flag pin lately. He's got a funny name. He says he's Christian, but we don't know. His former pastor said some terrible things and so, can we really trust this guy?"[68]

The small audience replied, "Yes!" At a campaign stop, a man asked about trade and then added, "I've been reading on the Internet that you believe as an American we should not have to pledge allegiance to the flag. Is that true?" Barack responded,

> It is not. That is completely bogus. These emails have been sent around in each state I'm about to go into. It's a smear campaign they've been running since the beginning of the campaign. I lead the Pledge of Allegiance when I'm presiding in the Senate.

An eighty-seven-year-old woman at a retirement center said she felt questions about Barack's religion, patriotism, and values were an excuse, adding, "I think there's a certain percentage of people who won't vote for him because he's black, and I think that's a shame.... I'm leaning toward him. How could you not?"[69]

Barack has said,

> I look forward as president to going before the world community and saying, "America is back. We're ready to lead.... " Because if you elect me, you will have elected a president who has taught the Constitution, who believes in the Constitution, and who will restore and obey the Constitution of the United States of America.[70]

On May 14, 2008, former presidential candidate Senator John Edwards endorsed Barack. He said,

> The reason I am here tonight is that Democratic voters in America have made their choice and so have I. There is one man who knows in his heart that it is time to create one America—not two—and that man is Barack Obama.[71]

On May 19, 2008, West Virginia's Senator Robert Byrd announced his endorsement for Barack. He said,

> After a great deal of thought, consideration and prayer over the situation in Iraq, I have decided that, as a superdelegate to the Democratic National Convention, I will cast my vote for Senator Barack Obama for President. Both Senators Clinton and Obama are extraordinary individuals, who integrity, honor, love for this country and strong belief in our Constitution I deeply respect. I believe Barack Obama is a shining young statesman, who possesses the personal temperament and courage necessary to extricate our country from this costly misadventure in Iraq, and to lead our nation at this challenging time in history. Barack Obama is a noble-hearted patriot and humble Christian, and he has my full faith and support.[72]

Michael Gerson wrote in the *Washington Post,*

> Obama is a serious, thoughtful, decent adult who will attract the sympathy of other serious, thoughtful decent adults. He has evident flaws, but the inspiration he evokes is genuine. His policy views are

conventionally liberal, but his story is not a scam. And, in some ways, his election would finally make sense of an American story that includes Antietam and Selma.[73]

One group of voters who were unsure of Barack and his campaign were some Jewish voters. Speaking before a group of Jewish voters in Florida on May 23, 2008, Barack said,

The bottom line is this. Nobody can find any statement that I have ever made that is anything less than unequivocally pro-Israel, that says Israel's security is paramount. There is not a single trace of me ever being anything more than a friend of Israel and a friend of the Jewish people. This is part, I think, of the tradition of the Jewish people is to judge me by what I say and what I have done. Don't judge me because I have a funny name. Don't judge me because I am an African-American. People are concerned about memories of the past … that is exactly what I am fighting in the African-American community when I hear anti-Semitic statements. We are bigger than that. If my policies are wrong, then vote against me because my policies are wrong. If I am not honest, if I am not truthful, don't vote for me for that reason. But don't vote against me because of who I am, and I know you won't.[74]

What would the first hundred days of an Obama administration look like? Barack responded to that question with the following:

Step number one is moving to end this war in Iraq … step two would be to put forth a bold plan for universal health care … the third is energy independence … if we take these steps then I'm confident that we can get this country back on track.[75]

In an article that appeared in *The New American*, author Gregory Hession described Barack as a "Man of the Government." The article points out that most everyone looks at the government in one of two ways: one group wants government to do something for them, whereas the other group seeks either to have government stop doing something to them or taking something from them. Barack, the article notes, came from political obscurity and wants to be the next president so he can run the government and asks what he believes and what are his core values. From his two books, *The Audacity of Hope* and *Dreams from My Father,* there is insight that answers these questions. Before and during his presidential bid, Barack has provided a reliable record of his beliefs and their historical development. Barack said, "My job is to inspire people to take ownership of this country. Politics is not a business. It's a mission. It's about making people's lives better." Barack is a man of the government. By taking, "ownership of this country," he does not mean limiting government to its constitutional size so that people can take care of themselves and manage their own lives; he means instead empowering government to manage the economy and provide for the people, thereby (in his view), "making people's lives better."[76]

The Concerns and Criticisms of Barack Obama and His Campaign for the Presidency

I am anxious to meet him. I want to see if he will walk the walk.

> Rupert Murdoch, chairman of News Corp., on Barack Obama, predicting his victory in November.[77]

A *New York Times* article in March 2004 was titled "As Quickly as Overnight, a Democratic Star Is Born." The article was written just after his successful bid for the U.S. Senate, a race he was expected to lose but instead won overwhelmingly. Prior to this win and prior to his speech at the Democratic National Convention, Barack had drawn little notice outside of his home state of Illinois. As quickly as nearly overnight, it seemed, Barack found himself on covers of magazines, the subject of countless articles around the country, and was constantly sought out for interviews and appearances. Before he had even been sworn in as the junior senator from Illinois, the rumors caught fire of whether he would run for president in 2012. It was not long before there was speculation that he would run in the 2008 election and the questions included: Was he electable? Was it his time? Was it too soon? Was he experienced enough? Would American voters elect an African American as president? Would women vote for Barack, or would they vote for Senator Clinton? Could he unite a divided country? Many asked, who is this tall, lanky man from Illinois that became only the third black American to hold a seat in the U.S. Senate since Reconstruction? Why is he so popular? Are the huge crowds to see a man who became as popular as some rock stars real? Are the people attending the rallies there to listen and do they really believe in his message of hope and change? Is he too liberal? Is he an elitist and can he identify with the middle class? Why isn't he wearing a flag pin on his lapel? Does he really refuse to say the Pledge of Allegiance? Was his hand on a Koran and not a Bible at his swearing in ceremony? Is he a Muslim or a Christian? Are terrorists really endorsing him? Is he patriotic, or not? Does he love his country and is he really of mixed race heritage? Is he black enough? What about his elect-ability? These questions, and many more, swirled about Barack through-out his campaign and he found himself deflecting the criticisms, explaining his views, and denouncing his pastor, and eventually leaving his home church. Still, he stayed with his message and never lost his cool.

On Race, on His Electability, and the Electorate

In an interview with the *Chicago Tribune* in June 2005, Barack was asked if America was ready for a black president and Barack answered: "Yea, I think an African-American candidate, if he's the best candidate, can be president."[78]

Jonathan Alter, writer for *Newsweek*, wrote an article entitled "Is America Ready?" in December 2006. Alter notes that Barack says the American people are looking for something new, but Alter asks, how new? For 220 years, he writes, Americans have elected only white male Christians with no hint of ethnicity to the White House. He also dis-cussed the prospect of electing the first woman as president and wrote that although no analysts say electing a woman president is impossible, some still make that case about a black candidate. Lawrence Otis Graham, an African American author, is quoted in the article:

There's a willingness to be entertained by African-Americans, but to be governed by them is a completely different story. White men have socialized and worked under women, but much more rarely under blacks. Whatever they say, when they go in the polling place, they won't go for it.

Alter wrote that Barack has no military service to deepen his connection to core American values; he also suggested that Barack's biggest challenge might be meeting such high expectations, and that some Democrats may be disappointed. When he gives a speech that is policy-heavy and lower in key in his rhetoric, some in the audience expect the (2004 Democratic) convention style oratory and may leave underwhelmed.[79]

In the same issue of *Newsweek,* Jonathan Alter interviewed Barack. Noting that there have been two African American governors and three senators since Reconstruction, he asked if America ready for a black or a woman president? Barack answered,

I absolutely think America is ready for either. Stereotypes and prejudices still exist in American society ... but what I've found is that the American people—once they get to know you—are going to judge you on your individual character.[80]

In an interview with Steve Kroft on CBS's *60 Minutes* in February 2007, Kroft asked if Barack was surprised and disappointed with Senator Clinton's lead among African American voters. Barack answered,

I think there is an assumption on the part of some commentators that somehow, the black community is so unsophisticated that the minute you put an African-American face up on the screen, that they automatically say, "That's our guy." A black candidate has to earn black votes the same way that he's gotta earn white votes. And—and that's exactly how it should be.[81]

The July 16, 2007 issue of *Newsweek's* cover story was "Black and White, How Barack Obama Is Shaking Up Old Assumptions." The magazine's article, "Across the Divide," noted one measure of Barack's broad support is his extraordinary fundraising. More than 150,000 donors gave $31 million for his primary campaign in the second quarter (2007), roughly $10 million more than Senator Clinton and far

Democratic presidential nominee Senator Barack Obama shakes hands after appearing with Senator Hillary Clinton, Democrat of New York, in Unity, New Hampshire on June 27, 2008, during their first joint public appearance since the divisive Democratic primary race ended. (AP Photo/Alex Brandon)

ahead of anyone else in either party. According to *Newsweek*, polls suggested that race is no longer the barrier it once was to electing a president. A clear majority—59 percent—said the country is ready to elect an African American president, up from 37 percent at the start of the decade; it still indicates that a significant percentage of the country is either skeptical or prejudiced. The article notes that Barack faced many challenges in what he calls his "improbable candidacy," but few are as complex or emotional as race, with racial politics a key source of his campaign's energy, and possibly his undoing. The question asked was could Barack appeal to both black and white, while still being true to himself?[82]

Drawing a sharp contrast with his rival, Senator Clinton, Barack said in August 2007 that he has the capacity she may lack to unify the country and move it out of what he called an "ideological gridlock." Barack said, "I think it is fair to say that I believe I can bring the country together more effectively than she can … if I didn't believe that, I wouldn't be running." Barack defended himself against criticisms from Hillary Clinton and other Democratic rivals with a series of statements on foreign policy and argued that her foreign policy views risked continued international perceptions of U.S. arrogance.

> Her argument is going to be that "I'm the experienced Washington hand," and my argument is going to be that we need to change the ways of Washington. That's going to be a good choice for the American people…. I don't think there is anybody in this race who's able to bring new people into the process and break out of some of the ideological gridlock that we have as effectively as I can.

Barack conceded that because many Democrats do not know him as well as they know Clinton, and that she was drawing more support nationally. "We've got to really fill in the blanks with folks, and that's going to be the challenge.[83]

From the beginning of the campaign season, from the first caucus in Iowa that Barack won handily, to the first primary in New Hampshire in which Hillary Clinton won with 39 percent of the vote to Barack's 36 percent, there were questions about how the voters would cast their ballots. It was more than voting for the first woman candidate and the first African American candidate. There were also other variations of voters including income, class, ethnicity, and geographical differences. By mid-February 2008, Barack emerged as the leader in the pledged delegates and it appeared that it would be difficult for Hillary Clinton to achieve the required number of delegates to surpass him with the remaining primary and caucuses through June. However, it also appeared that neither candidate would have the required number of pledged delegates needed to claim the nomination by the time voting would end with the last primary scheduled for June 7, 2008. Questions were emerging about how voters would cast their vote and whether Barack could appeal to blue-collar workers, the middle class, Hispanics, women, and seniors. Polls showed Hillary fared better within these voter categories, and Barack did well with African Americans, younger voters, and upper-income voters. Both candidates were showing strength in every region of the country. No one disputed the fact that more voters were casting ballots than ever before and Democrats were enjoying an energized electorate and donations were flowing into both campaigns in record numbers. From the first contests, it appeared that it would be a state-by-state battle until the very end of the campaign season.

By March 2008, political pundits were questioning why Barack couldn't "close the deal" with his lead in pledged delegates and his massive fundraising. Barack lost in the Ohio and Texas primaries to Clinton, after appearing nearly invincible the week before. He faced questions about his toughness and his vulnerabilities, although he was still attracting huge crowds at his speeches and enjoying record-setting fundraising. Despite the crowds and donations to his campaign, polls showed he was having difficulty attracting working-class and middle-class support. Barack noted,

> I don't buy into this demographic argument. In Missouri, Wisconsin, Virginia, and many of these states, we've won the white vote and the blue-collar voters. I think it is very important not to somehow focus on a handful of states because the Clintons say that those states are important and the other states are unimportant.[84]

The question was then asked if Barack was ready to be president and if he had passed the "commander-in-chief test." A spokesman for the Clinton campaign suggested that Barack was not ready to be president, and that despite Barack's lead in the delegate count and primary and caucus wins thus far, he should consider being vice president to Hillary's presidency. Barack noted in a speech in Mississippi on March 11, 2008, on the day of that state's primary, that he had won more delegates, more of the popular vote, had won twice as many states as Hillary, and said he didn't understand, "how it is if I'm not ready, how do you think I can be such a great vice-president?"[85]

With the campaign looking as if it would go on until the last primary in early June 2008, both candidates looked to define what it meant to be winning. Barack emphasized the breadth of his appeal with his lead in the popular vote and pledged delegates and victories in states that Democrats had trouble carrying in prior elections. Hillary focused on her victories in states with the highest number of electoral votes, like

Ohio and California, and her strength among women, blue-collar workers, and Hispanics. Hillary lost in the Mississippi Primary, stating it was because half of the voters in the primary were black. In that state, nine in ten blacks voted for Barack and 40% of voters told pollsters that race was a factor in their decision. Adding fuel to the criticisms, the questions about both campaigns, and to the question of race and whether whites would vote for Barack, Geraldine A. Ferraro, the former New York representative and a Clinton supporter, suggested that Barack's success was in part due to his race. She told the California paper, *Daily Breeze*, "If Obama was a white man, he would not be in this position." Barack stated he was outraged at the remark. Ms. Ferraro resigned from her capacity as a fundraiser for the Clinton campaign; however, she continued to stand by her statement. The March 15, 2008 issue of *The Economist* noted that Barack had won a majority of white votes in states with different demographics such as Virginia, New Mexico, Wisconsin, Illinois, Utah, and in Wyoming, where 90 percent of the population is white.[86]

On April 6, 2008, at a fundraiser in San Francisco, California, Barack made comments that set off a political firestorm. Trying to explain his troubles at winning over some working-class voters, Barack said that many of these voters had become frustrated with economic conditions. He said, "It's not surprising, then, they get bitter, they cling to guns or religion or antipathy to people who aren't like them or anti-immigrant sentiment or anti-trade sentiment as a way to explain their frustrations." His comments were posted on *The Huffington Post* website and subsequently set off a blast of criticism from the Clinton campaign, as well as from John McCain, the Republican presumptive nominee. Barack's campaign scrambled to diffuse the fall out from his remarks and he tried to apologize by saying he worded things in a way that offended people and he deeply regretted it. The Clinton campaign noted that Barack's remarks showed he was an elitist, charges that had been previously leveled against Barack, and that he was arrogant and out of touch with voters, especially in states like Pennsylvania, Ohio, and Indiana. On a campaign stop in Muncie, Indiana prior to the Indiana Primary, Barack said there had been a flare up because of something he said that

> everybody knows is true, which is that there are a whole bunch of folks in small towns in Pennsylvania, in towns right here in Indiana,

in my hometown in Illinois, who are bitter. They are angry. They feel like they have been left behind. They feel like nobody is paying attention to what they're going through. So I said ... when you're bitter you turn to what you can count on. So people, they vote about guns, or they take comfort from their faith and their family and their community. And they get mad about illegal immigrants who are coming over to this country.

Hillary Clinton responded: "People don't need a president who looks down on them. They need a president who stands up for them."[87]

On April 19, 2008, former Labor Secretary Robert Reich became the fifth former Clinton cabinet member to endorse Barack, saying that loyalty to his old friends, the Clintons, had been overwhelmed by unhappiness with the tone of the Clinton campaign.

I did not plan to endorse. I wanted to stay out of the whole endorsement racket. But my conscience wouldn't let me stay silent after this latest round of mudslinging. When millions of Americans are losing their homes and jobs, when the economy is facing its worst crisis in 60 years, when the Iraq war is still causing chaos in the Middle East, to focus on whether Obama should have used the word "bitter" when he talked about the plight of many in Pennsylvania, and to resurrect the old Republican themes of guns and religion, and to call Obama "elitist"... just put me over the edge.[88]

A continuing controversy that seemed to surround Barack during the campaign was the fact that he did not wear a flag pin on his suit lapel. To some, by not wearing the symbol, it meant he was unpatriotic and led to the question of whether Barack loved America. Early on in the campaign, he told an audience in Iowa,

My attitude is that I'm less concerned about what you're wearing on your lapel than what's in your heart. You show your patriotism by how you treat your fellow Americans, especially those who served. You show your patriotism by being true to our values and our ideals.

The controversy seemed to die down for a while, until Barack started winning more nominating contests. Then it dogged him again in Ohio, Texas, Pennsylvania, and in Indiana. In May 2008, Barack called it a "phony issue" and that he was not opposed to wearing flag pins. "It was a commentary on our politicians and folks in Washington who sometimes are very good about saluting our soldiers when they come home, but then don't follow up with budgets that make sure they're getting treatment for post-traumatic stress disorder."[89]

On His Experience and the Issues

In a debate of presidential candidates, Barack said he was willing to meet with Fidel Castro, Kim Jung Il, and Hugo Chavez separately and without preconditions during his first year as president. A few months later, he was asked on NBC's *Meet the Press* if he stood by his answer and he said that he did.

> I did not say that I would be meeting with all of them. I said I'd be willing to. Obviously there is a difference between preconditions and preparation. Preconditions, which was what the question was in that debate, means that we won't meet with people unless they've already agreed to the very things that we expect to be meeting with them about.

When he was asked about being used in a propaganda way, Barack said, "Strong countries and strong presidents speak with their adversaries. I always think back to JFK's saying that we should never negotiate out of fear, but we shouldn't fear to negotiate."[90]

In an article entitled "The Obama Factor," James Pindell, who covers presidential primary politics for the *Boston Globe*, wrote in December 2006, "He has zero credentials on foreign policy, one of the most important issues in 2008. And he is relatively untested as a candidate and an executive."[91]

Barack discussed the question of his experience in December 2006.

> I think that experience question would be answered during the course of the campaign. Either at the end of that campaign, people would say, "He looked good on paper but the guy was kind of way too green" or at the end of the campaign they say, "He's run a really strong campaign and we think he's got something to say and we think he could lead us."[92]

According to *The Economist* magazine in June 2007,

An Obama presidency would carry great symbolic weight … would signal to many, in and outside America, that the American dream still works. His opposition to the two policies that have hurt America's image most—invading Iraq and making use of torture—will convince many that he represents a fresh start. But his inexperience is worrisome, and the source of Mrs. Clinton's greatest advantage over him. He is decent, intelligent and a good listener. But as George Will, a conservative columnist, put it, he is asking Americans to "treat the presidency as a nearly entry-level political office." Mr. Obama once cruelly pointed out that experience is what Dick Cheney and Donald Rumsfeld have plenty of. Yet it still counts for something, after all.[93]

At just forty-six years old and three years out of the Illinois legislature, as the freshman senator from Illinois, Barack understood that the clock was ticking on his chance to convince voters that he is ready for the White House. "The challenge for us is to let people know what I've accomplished at a time when the campaign schedule is getting so compressed. I just don't have much time to make that case." He promised to bring change to a political system that most voters think is broken:

People have to feel comfortable that, "You know what? This guy can handle the job." It's a stretch for them because I haven't been on the national scene for long and haven't gone through the conventional paths that we traditionally draw for our president.… I think it's fair that I've got to earn the confidence of the electorate. What we've tried to do over the course of the last six months is make the case for change. The next four or five or six months will involve me making the case that not only am I the most effective change agent but I'm also equipped with the experience and judgment to be the next commander in chief.[94]

In October 2007, Barack was still lagging behind Hillary Clinton in the polls, despite raising money faster than any other Democrat, despite being a fresh, attractive face and an inspirational message; his candidacy seemed to be idling. Part of the problem, according to Karen Tumulty of *Time*, was his low-key speaking delivery. Said one advisor of a rival campaign, "His style is so cerebral and so cool that it just doesn't appeal to a wide segment of the Democratic Party. They want to like him, but he just isn't connecting with them." An unaffiliated campaign strategist said, "His is a subtle and nuanced campaign, and this is not a subtle and nuanced business."[95]

The December 15, 2007 *The Economist* asked the question of whether hope could triumph over experience:

> He [Barack] has always been the candidate of "hope." As America's first black president, he would show a new face to the world.... He appeals to Republican voters far more than other Democrats.... A President Obama would turn preconceptions upside down: indeed he might be able to achieve far more both at home and abroad than any other candidate. But hope does not balance budgets, craft alliances or reform schools. It certainly does not prove that Mr. Obama would be the best, or even a good, president. Mr. Obama cannot change his experience deficit; but he can change his substance deficit.... Offering America a chance to heal its divisions is a powerful selling point ... but it is not enough. Mr. Obama still needs to do more to show how he defines change, as opposed just to personifying it.[96]

President Bill Clinton told Charlie Rose on *The Charlie Rose Show*, that picking Obama "is a roll of the dice" and that sometimes Barack seems more concerned with process than results.[97]

On His Faith and the Reverend Jeremiah Wright

In early March 2007, a month after his announcement to run for the presidency, Barack attended a celebration to honor the long service of Reverend Jeremiah A. Wright, Jr. as the pastor of the Trinity United Church of Christ. As a presidential candidate, he certainly stood out in the crowd to honor the man he said led him from skeptic to self-described Christian twenty years before. Few in the crowd understood the pressures that Barack's presidential run was placing on his relationship with the pastor. The Reverend's assertions of widespread white racism and his remarks about the government have drawn criticism, and those assertions and remarks caused the cancellation of the Reverend's invocation at Barack's February announcement to run for president. When questioned about his decision not to have the Reverend speak in Springfield that day, Barack said in April 2007 that he was only shielding his pastor from the spotlight and that he respected Reverend Wright's work for the poor and his fight against injustice, adding that he and Wright did not agree on everything and that he'd never had a thorough conversation with him about all aspects of politics.

Barack's pastor and his association with him and the church became a lightning rod during Barack's campaign. It became known that on the Sunday after the attacks on September 11, 2001, Wright said the attacks were a consequence of violent American politics. Four years later, he wrote that the attacks had proved that "people of color had not gone away, faded into the woodwork or just 'disappeared' as the Great White West went on its merry way of ignoring Black concerns." Michael Cromartie, vice president of Ethics and Public Policy Center, a group that studies religious issues and public policy, said such statements involved "a certain deeply embedded anti-Americanism. A lot of people are going to say to Mr. Obama, are those your views?" Barack said they were not, "The violence of 9/11 was inexcusable and without justification," and added that he was not at the Trinity church the day Wright delivered his remarks.

> Reverend Wright is a child of the 60s, and he often expresses himself in that language of concern with institutional racism and the struggles the African-American community has gone through. He analyzes public events in the context of race. I tend to look at them through the context of social justice and inequality.

When asked about the cancellation of the invocation in February, Wright said he has long prided himself on criticizing the establishment, and said he knew he might not play well in Barack's audition for the ultimate establishment job. He said, "If Barack gets past the primary, he might have to publicly distance himself from me. I said it to Barack personally, and he said yeah, that might have to happen."[98]

The issue of Barack's pastor, Reverend Jeremiah Wright came up again and again during the campaign. His fiery, divisive remarks made during his sermons at Barack's home church appeared on YouTube and caused such a sensation that the story was picked up and reported on by the mainstream news and was part of the news cycles for days on end. Barack found himself having to deflect comments about his association with the pastor's fiery rhetoric and being a member of the church for more than twenty years. The question was asked if Barack heard the sermons, why had he not denounced them or walked out of the church during the sermons, and if he disagreed with the expressed sentiment and why would he not denounce the pastor. Barack struggled to distance himself from Wright for nearly a week after the comments surfaced that characterized the United States as fundamentally racist and the government as corrupt and murderous.

On March 18, 2008, Barack made a speech at the National Constitution Center in Philadelphia, a building steeped in the nation's historic symbolism. The speech was described as a sweeping assessment of race in America and some likened its importance to that of Martin Luther King's "I Have a Dream" speech. Barack declared in the speech that it was time for America to move beyond some of the old racial wounds:

It's a racial stalemate we've been stuck in for years. Contrary to the claims of some of my critics, black and white, I have never been so naïve as to believe that we can get beyond our racial divisions in a single election cycle, or with a single candidacy—particularly a candidacy as imperfect as my own.

The speech was one of the most extensive of Barack's presidential campaign devoted to race and unity and what some declared was one of the biggest tests of his candidacy. Barack disavowed the remarks by his pastor as "not only wrong, but divisive, divisive at a time when we need unity." He did not, however, wholly distance himself from his pastor or the church. He said,

I can no more disown him than I disown the black community. I can no more disown him than I can disown my white grandmother—a woman who helped raise me, a woman who sacrificed again and again for me, a woman who loves me as much as she loves anything in this world, but a woman who once confessed her fear of black men who passed by her on the street, and who on more than one occasion has uttered racial or ethnic stereotypes that made me cringe.

Standing against a backdrop of American flags, Barack described his association with the church and the pastor:

> For some, nagging questions remain. Did I know him to be an occasionally fierce critic of American domestic and foreign policy? Of course. Did I ever hear him make remarks that could be considered controversial while I sat in church? Yes. Did I strongly disagree with many of his political views? Absolutely—just as I'm sure many of you have heard remarks from your pastors, priests or rabbis with which you strongly disagreed.

Speaking for nearly forty-five minutes, Barack continued to say that race is an issue he believed the nation cannot afford to ignore and that the safe thing would be to move on and hope that the issue faded. He said he has seen how people in America were hoping for a message of unity and that despite the temptation to view his candidacy through a purely racial lens, he reminded everyone of his victories in states with some of the whitest populations in the country. Barack added,

> The comments that have been made and the issues that have surfaced over the last few weeks reflect the complexities of race in this country that we've never really worked through—a part of our union that we have not yet made perfect. And if we walk away now, if we simply retreat into our respective corners, we will never be able to come together and solve challenges like health care, or education or the need to find good jobs for every American.[99]

At the end of the speech, Barack said,

> We can play Reverend Wright's sermons on every channel, every day and talk about them from now until the election, and make the only question in this campaign whether or not the American people think that I somehow believe or sympathize with his most offensive words … we can do that. But if we do, I can tell you that in the next election, we'll be talking about some other distraction. And then another one … and nothing will change. That is one option. Or, at this moment, in

this election, we can come together and say, "Not this time...." I would not be running for President if I didn't believe with all my heart that this is what the vast majority of Americans want for this country. This union may never be perfect, but generation after generation has shown that it can always be perfected. And today, whenever I find myself feeling doubtful or cynical about this possibility, what gives me the most hope is the next generation—the young people who attitudes and beliefs and openness to change have already made history in this election.[100]

Joe Klein, columnist for *Time*, wrote about the speech:

> The rhetorical magic of the speech—what made it extraordinary—was that it was, at once, both unequivocal and healing.... Obama was unequivocal in his candor about black anger and white resentment—sentiments that few mainstream politicians acknowledge.... It was a grand demonstration of the largely unfulfilled promise of Obama's candidacy: the possibility that, given his eloquence and intelligence, he will be able to create a new sense of national unity—not by smoothing over problems but by confronting them candidly and with civility.[101]

Klein noted that most Americans would hear the speech in sound bytes and from headlines and from that would only hear that Barack had refused to denounce or disavow his pastor and the Wright controversy was the third many had heard about Barack and candidacy, with the first him being black and the second, that he had a "funny" name. He suggested that too many voters do not go beyond their first impressions and noted that this is the challenge for 2008, whether the election will be a big one or small one, whether there will be serious conversations about the enormous problems facing the country—the wars, the economy, the environment—or would there be only the sound bites as in past elections, where cynicism passes for insight.

On April 29, 2008, showing more emotion than was typical for him, Barack held a press conference to fully denounce Reverend Jeremiah Wright after the pastor's remarks made at a National Press Club speech on April 28. In addition to defending his plea that "God damn America," Reverend Wright also made accusations that the U.S. government had unleashed HIV/AIDS on the African American community and engaged in "terrorism" overseas. Barack said,

I am outraged by the comments that were made and saddened over the spectacle that we saw yesterday. I have been a member of Trinity United Church of Christ since 1992. I have known Reverend Wright for almost 20 years. The person I saw yesterday wasn't the person that I met 20 years ago. The comments weren't only divisive and destructive. I believe that they end up giving comfort to those who prey on hate. I believe they don't portray accurately the perspective of the black church. They certainly don't portray accurately my values and beliefs. And if Reverend Wright thinks that is political posturing, as he put it, then he doesn't know me very well. And based on his remarks yesterday, I may not know him as well as I thought, either.

Barack said what had become clear to him was more than Wright defending himself, but what he said presented a worldview that contradicts what Barack stood for. Barack suggested he was considering leaving the church, but had yet to speak to the pastor of the church, Reverend Otis Moss, about his position. He said that when he goes to church, it is not for spectacle, but rather it is to pray and find a stronger sense of faith. He added it was not to posture politically and not to hear things that violated his core beliefs.[102]

On May 31, 2008, Barack formally announced that he had resigned his membership of the Trinity United Church of Christ, where he had attended for nearly two decades, following the months of controversy about his pastor and his political views. In a letter sent to the church and the current pastor from both Barack and his wife Michelle, they said,

Our relations with Trinity have been strained by the divisive statements of Reverend Wright, which sharply conflict with our own views. These controversies have served as an unfortunate distraction for other Trinity members who seek to worship in peace, and have placed you in an untenable position.

In a town-hall-style meeting in Aberdeen, South Dakota, Barack sounded pained as he confirmed his decision to leave the church that had been his spiritual home. He told the audience, "I make this decision with sadness. This is where I found Jesus Christ, where we were married, where our children were baptized. We are proud of the extraordinary works of that church." Barack rejected suggestions that he also denounce the church, stating that he was not interested in people who wanted him to denounce it and that it was not a church worthy of denouncing.[103]

NOTES

1. Jeff Zeleny, "The First Time Around: Senator Obama's Freshman Year," *Chicago Tribune,* December 24, 2005, http://www.chicagotribune.com/news/local/chi-051224obama,0,6232648.story (accessed May 20, 2008).
2. Amanda Griscom Little, "Barack Obama," *Rolling Stone,* December 30, 2004, 88.
3. Ryan Lizza, "Above the Fray," *GQ,* September 2007, 334.
4. Evan Thomas, Holly Bailey, and Richard Wolffe "Only in America," *Newsweek,* May 5, 2008, 28.
5. Liza Mundy, "A Series of Fortunate Events," *Washington Post,* August 12, 2007, W10.
6. Marc Ambinder, "Teacher and Apprentice," *The Atlantic,* December 2007, 59.
7. Ken Rudin, "Obama, or a History of Black Presidents of the U.S.," *National Public Radio,* December 7, 2006.
8. Marc Ambinder, "Teacher and Apprentice," *The Atlantic,* December 2007, 59.
9. Ibid., 60.
10. Gwen Ifill, "On the Road with Michelle," *Essence,* September 2007.
11. Rudin, "Obama, or a History of Black Presidents of the U.S."
12. Steve Dougherty, *Hopes and Dreams, the Story of Barack Obama* (New York: Black Dog & Leventhal Publishers, Inc., 2007), 104.
13. Byron York, "Obama Madness," *National Review,* November 20, 2006, 17–18.
14. Adam Nagourney and Jeff Zeleny, "Obama Formally Enters Presidential Race with Calls for Generational Change," *New York Times,* February 11, 2007, 22.
15. Ibid.
16. Jonathan Clayton and Nyangoma Kogela, "Favourite Son Is Already a Winner in Kenya," *Times of London,* February 10, 2007.
17. Ambinder, "Teacher and Apprentice," 64.
18. Richard Wolffe and Even Thomas, "Sit Back, Relax, Get Ready to Rumble," *Newsweek,* May 19, 2008, 21.
19. Ambinder, "Teacher and Apprentice," 64.
20. Rick Klein and Nancy Flores, "The Note: Double-Oh Show," *ABC News Online,* December 7, 2007, http://abcnews.com (accessed December 7, 2007).
21. "Obama's Moment," *The Economist,* December 1, 2007, 46.
22. Jeremy Pelofsky, "Sen. Obama Nears Clinton in Campaign Money Race," *Reuters,* April 4, 2007.
23. Zeleny, "The First Time Around."
24. Rick Pearson, "Obama on Obama," *Chicago Tribune,* December 15, 2006, http://www.chicagotribune.com (accessed May 19, 2008).
25. Peggy Noonan, "The Man from Nowhere," *Wall Street Journal,* December 16, 2006, 14.
26. Karen E. Crummy, "Obama: "The Country Calls Us," *Denver Post,* March 19, 2007, 5B.
27. Jeff Zeleny, "Testing the Water: Obama Tests His Own Limits," *New York Times,* December 24, 2006, 1.1.

28. Perry Bacon, Jr., "The Exquisite Dilemma of Being Obama," *Time,* February 20, 2006, 24.

29. Ryan Grim, "Obama's World," *The Politico,* March 6, 2007, http://www.politico.com (accessed March 6, 2007).

30. Bacon, Jr., "The Exquisite Dilemma of Being Obama."

31. David Remnick, "Testing the Waters," *New Yorker,* November 6, 2006, http://www.newyorker.com (accessed May 19, 2008).

32. Zeleny, "Testing the Water."

33. Barack Obama, "Interview by Steve Kroft." *60 Minutes,* February 11, 2007, http://www.il.proquest.com (accessed May 19, 2008).

34. Mike Allen and Ben Smith, "Liberal Views Could Haunt Obama," *USA Today,* December 12, 2007, http://www.usatoday.com (accessed December 12, 2007).

35. Barack Obama, "February 12 Speech," *New York Times,* February 12, 2008.

36. Adam Nagourney, "Surging, Obama Makes His Case," *New York Times,* February 13, 2008.

37. Dougherty, *Hopes and Dreams,* 108.

38. Mundy, "A Series of Fortunate Events."

39. Jason Szep and Ellen Wulfhorst, "Undecided Voters Give Obama Hope in 2008 Race," *Reuters News,* November 21, 2007.

40. Jim Spencer, "Obama Needs Inspiration to Get His Optimism Across," *Denver Post,* March 19, 2007.

41. York, "Obama Madness," 17–18.

42. Jonathan Alter, "Is America Ready?" *Newsweek,* December 25, 2006, 28–35.

43. Ruth Marcus, "The Clintonian Candidate," *Washington Post,* January 31, 2007, A15.

44. Kenneth T. Walsh, "Talkin' 'Bout My New Generation," *U.S. News & World Report,* January 8, 2007, 26–28.

45. Ibid.

46. Andrew Sullivan, "Goodbye to All That," *The Atlantic,* December 2007, 46, 48.

47. Eugene Robinson, "The Moment for This Messenger?" *Washington Post,* March 13, 2007, A17.

48. Larissa MacFarquhar, "The Conciliator," *The New Yorker,* May 7, 2007.

49. Lizza, "Above the Fray," 337.

50. Anne E. Kornblut and Shailagh Murray, "I'm Tired of Politics as Usual," *Washington Post,* December 9, 2007, A01.

51. Nedra Pickler, "Winfrey, Clinton Kin Draw Crowds of Iowa Women," *Denver Post,* December 9, 2007, 8a.

52. Jason Clayworth, "Obama Victory Speech: 'Time for Change has Come,' " *Des Moines Register,* January 4, 2008, http://www.desmoinesregister.com (accessed January 4, 2008).

53. Lydia Gensheimer, "Big Crowd, Big Win for Obama in Heart of Des Moines," *CQ Today,* January 4, 2008.

54. David Brooks, "The Two Earthquakes," *New York Times,* January 4, 2008.

55. "Obamamania," *The Economist,* January 12, 2008, 26.

56. Barack Obama, "Concession Speech," http://thepage.time.com, January 9, 2008.

57. Adam Nagourney, "Obama Made Inroads, but Fervor Fell Short," *New York Times,* February 7, 2008, http://www.msnbc.msn.com (accessed February 7, 2008).

58. "A Fighter in Search of an Opponent," *The Economist,* February 9, 2008, 30.
59. "Republicans for Obama," *The Nation,* February 25, 2008, http://www.thenation. com (accessed February 26, 2008).
60. Jonathan Alter, "Obama Plays Offense," *Newsweek,* February 4, 2008, 32.
61. Michael Powell and Jeff Zeleny, "Lesson of Defeat: Obama Comes out Punching," *New York Times,* March 6, 2008, A1.
62. Tom Baldwin and Tim Reid, "I'm Winning This Race, Barack Obama Says, So Why Should I Be No 2?" *Times Online,* March 11, 2008, http://www.timesonline. co.uk (accessed March 11, 2008).
63. "On the Campaign Trail, Primary Colour," *The Economist,* March 15, 2008, 38.
64. Jeff Zeleny, "Obama Wins in Mississippi," *New York Times,* March 12, 2008, http://www.nytimes.com (accessed March 12, 2008).
65. Katharine Q. Seelye, "The Casey Endorsement," *New York Times,* March 28, 2008, http://www.nytimes.com (accessed March 28, 2008).
66. John Harwood, "In Superdelegate Count, Tough Math for Clinton," *New York Times,* April 7, 2008, A.18.
67. Jeff Zeleny and John M. Broder, "On Eve of Primary, Clinton Ad Invokes bin Laden," *New York Times,* April 22, 2008, A.23.
68. Jeff Zeleny, "Obama Leaves the Stage to Mix with His Skeptics," *New York Times,* May 2, 2008, A.17.
69. Ibid.
70. Charles P. Pierce, "The Cynic and Senator Obama," *Esquire,* June 2008, 109.
71. Jim Rutenberg, "Edwards Finally Chooses a Favorite," *New York Times,* May 15, 2008, A.1.
72. Jeff Zeleny and Katharine Q. Seelye, "West Virginia's Byrd Supports Obama," *New York Times,* May 19, 2008, http://www.nytimes.com (accessed May 19, 2008).
73. Michael Gerson, "A Phenom with Flaws," *Washington Post,* May 23, 2008, http:// www.washingtonpost.com (accessed May 26, 2008).
74. Carrie Budoff Brown, "Obama Asks Jewish Voters for Chance," *Politico,* May 23, 2008, http://www.politico.com (accessed May 26, 2008).
75. Michael Williams, "One-On-One Interview with Barack Obama," *CBS,* May 23, 2008, http://cbs4.com/local/barack.obama.michael.2.731465.html (accessed May 26, 2008).
76. Gregory A. Hession, "Barack Obama," *The New American,* May 26, 2008, 22.
77. "Verbatim," *Time,* June 16, 2008, 12.
78. "Q & A with Senator Barack Obama," *Chicago Tribune,* June 30, 2005. General Reference Center Gold. Gale (accessed May 20, 2008).
79. Jonathan Alter, "Is America Ready?" *Newsweek,* December 25, 2006, 28–35.
80. Jonathan Alter, "The Challenges We Face," *Newsweek,* December 25, 2006, 36–40.
81. Steve Kroft, "Candidate Obama Feels 'Sense of Urgency,' " *60 Minutes,* February 11, 2007, http://www.il.proquest.com (accessed May 22, 2008).
82. Richard Wolffe and Daren Briscoe, "Across the Divide," *Newsweek,* July 16, 2007, 25.
83. Dan Balz, "Obama Says He Can Unite U.S. 'More Effectively' Than Clinton," *Washington Post,* August 15, 2007, A01.
84. Powell and Zeleny, "Lesson of Defeat."

85. Baldwin and Reid, "I'm Winning This Race."

86. "Getting Fratricidal," *The Economist,* March 15, 2008, 38.

87. Jim Kuhnhenn and Charles Babington, "Bitter" Words Spur Debate," *The Denver Post,* April 13, 2008, 21A.

88. Mark Z. Barabak, "Ex-Labor Secretary Reich Backs Obama," *Los Angeles Times,* April 19, 2008, http://www.latimes.com (accessed April 19, 2008).

89. Jim Rutenberg and Jeff Zeleny, "The Politics of the Lapel, When It Comes to Obama," *New York Times,* May 15, 2008. A.27.

90. "Barack Obama on Foreign Policy," http://www.ontheissues.org/International/Barack_Obama_Foreign_Policy.htm (accessed June 2, 2008).

91. James Pindell, "The Obama Factor," *Campaigns & Elections,* December 2006, 98.

92. Rick Pearson, "Obama on Obama," *Chicago Tribune,* December 15, 2006, http://www.il.proquest.com (accessed May 28, 2008).

93. "The Campaign's Brightest Star," *The Economist,* June 16, 2007, 34.

94. Ron Fournier, "Obama Presidency a 'Stretch' for Voters," *Associated Press,* August 21, 2007, http://abcnews.go.com (accessed August 21, 2007).

95. Karen Tumulty, "Out of Reach?" *Time,* October 8, 2007, 50, 52.

96. "The Triumph of Hope over Experience?" *The Economist,* December 15, 2007, 16–18.

97. David Brooks, "The Obama-Clinton Issue," *New York Times,* December 18, 2007, A.35.

98. Jodi Kantor, "A Candidate, His Minister and the Search for Faith," *New York Times,* April 30, 2007, A.1.

99. Jeff Zeleny, "Assessing Race in America, Obama Calls Pastor Divisive," *New York Times,* March 18, 2008, A.1.

100. Barack Obama, "A More Perfect Union," March 18, 2008, http://www.barackobama.com (accessed March 19, 2008).

101. Joe Klein, "Obama's Challenge—and Ours," *Time,* March 31, 2008, 31.

102. Richard Wolffe, "Obama's Sister Souljah Moment," *Newsweek,* April 29, 2008, http://www.newsweek.com (accessed April 29, 2008).

103. Michael Powell, "Following Months of Criticism, Obama Quits His Church," *New York Times,* June 1, 2008, http://www.nytimes.com (accessed June 2, 2008).

CHAPTER 6

On the Issues

"I believe it is time for a new generation to tell the next great American story. If we act with boldness and foresight, we will be able to tell our grandchildren that this was the time when we helped forge peace in the Middle East. This was the time we confronted climate change and secured the weapons that could destroy the human race. This was the time we defeated global terrorists and brought opportunity to forgotten corners of the world. And this was the time when we renewed the America that has led generations of weary travelers from all over the world to find opportunity and liberty and hope on our doorstep. We can be this America again. This is our moment to renew the trust and faith of our people—and all people—in an America that battles immediate evils, promotes an ultimate good, and leads the world once more."[1]

Introduction

Barack is known as an amazing orator. Even those who disagree with him often say that he knows how to give a great speech, that he is able to arouse a crowd, and that he can truly inspire hope in his audience. However, Barack has often been criticized by his admirers, supporters, the pundits, and political opponents that although he can turn an amazing phrase, that he uses "big words" and always seems to be able to get a crowd of any size clapping and chanting, he is not specific enough and does not take actual positions on the issues. As the 2008 campaign goes forward and he finds he must communicate with Democrats, Republicans, and the swing voters, unless he is very specific and his positions are clear, he may find the criticisms get louder and his supporters begin to wonder.

At a campaign stop in Denver in March 2007, Barack told the audience that he understood they no longer had confidence in their elected leaders and that they believed "government feels like a business instead

Democratic presidential nominee Senator Barack Obama waves to supporters before speaking at a primary night rally on June 3, 2008, in St. Paul, Minnesota. (AP Photo/Morry Gash)

of a mission." His campaign, he assured them, was their campaign, shouting, "We have to take over Washington. At every juncture when the people decided to change this country, it changed."[2] Touching on health care, education, and energy, Barack's biggest response came when he stated once again that the Iraq war should never have been authorized and added that America was less safe and America's standing in the world was diminished. A Denver man, standing near the stage, stated to the *Denver Post* reporter that he already knew he was backing Barack for president, stating, "He has soul and a conscience, and he's looking out for Joe Blow." A woman in the crowd, describing herself as a lifelong Republican, said she hadn't been happy with the current administration and after hearing Barack's speech, she liked what he said.[3]

The next day, a columnist for the *Denver Post* wrote that Barack would need ongoing inspiration to keep conveying his optimism to voters and wondered if Barack could continue to inspire after his short time on the campaign trail. In his article, he quoted a sixty-three-year-old man who had driven to Denver to hear Barack: "He gives me hope as a presidential candidate. He will win because the American public is ready for a change. He's energized people to a level I haven't seen since JFK and RFK." He wrote about a nineteen-year-old college student who said she wanted to vote for someone she could believe in, and of a fifty-nine-year-old woman who wanted to see Barack in person, adding that there was something about Barack that made her think she could trust him, that she thought the idea of being hopeful again was wonderful, and that she hadn't been that hopeful since 1968. The key, the columnist said, was for Barack to continue to inspire and to keep voters' attention. He agreed with an advertising salesman in the crowd: "He's timely. But as this thing goes on, he's got to get a lot more specific and a lot stronger."[4]

In November 2004, Barack spoke with Oprah Winfrey about his multicultural upbringing, his political plans, priorities, and the saving grace of his wife and daughters. Oprah asked him what he wanted to do with his politics. Barack answered,

> I want to make real the American ideal that every child in this country has a shot at life. Right now that's not true in the aggregate ... But so many kids have the odds stacked so high against them. The odds don't have to be that high. We can be sure that they start off

with health insurance, that they have early childhood education, that they have a roof over their heads, and that they have good teachers. These are things we can afford to do that will make a difference. Part of my task is to persuade the majority in this country that those investments are worth it, and if we make better choices in our government, we can deliver on that promise.[5]

Writing for *The Nation*, David Sirota interviewed Barack in his Capitol Hill office in June 2006. Sirota asked Barack to explain his "healthcare for hybrids" auto industry proposal and why not simply push to strengthen fuel-efficiency mandates. Barack answered,

> There is a difference between an opinion writer or thinker and a legislator. I a lot of times don't get an opportunity to frame legislation in ways that I would exactly prefer. I have to take into account what is possible within the constraints of the institution.

Fuel-efficiency standards, Barack said, provided a good example of what he was talking about. He said the two senators from Michigan, Levin and Stabenow, are progressive senators, but "if you have a conversation with them about standards, they are adamantly opposed. That's something that I've got to take into account if I'm going to be able to actually get something accomplished."[6]

> I would say, domestically, our national debt and budget constrain us in ways that are going to be very far-reaching, and long lasting ... I think whoever is elected in 2008 is going to be cleaning up the fiscal mess that was created as a consequence of the President's tax cuts ... the incapacity to take serious action around a set of issues that, if we don't deal with now, will leave us in either an uncompetitive position, in the case of energy, an environmental point of no return. It's the fact that we didn't get started on a whole host of issues that we shouldn't be starting right now, because it takes long lead times to change the schools, or it takes long lead times to develop alternative energy sources. I think those are years of missed opportunity that make it harder for us to deal with them in the future.[7]

Attempting to brush off the question of race in his campaign, Barack said in December 2007, "My job is to get known in this race.

African-American voters, Latino voters, women voters ... what they are concerned about is not identity, it's issues"[8]

In an address held in a football stadium in Columbia, South Carolina, an early voting state, Barack told a crowd estimated at 29,000, "I'm tired of Democrats thinking the only way to look tough on national security is to act like George Bush. We need a bold Democratic Party that's going to stand for something, not just posture and pose." Barack said if he is the party nominee, an opponent would not be able to say he supported going to war in Iraq. He added,

> It's not good enough to tell the people what you think they want to hear, instead of what they need to hear. That just won't do. Not this time. We can't spend all our time triangulating and poll-testing our positions because we're worried about what Mitt [Romney] or Fred [Thompson] or the other Republican nominees are going to say about us.[9]

In an interview with *Newsweek* magazine in February 2008, Barack was asked, "Even great presidents accomplish only two or three big things. What will you have accomplished at the end of eight years?" Barack answered,

> We will have ended the war in Iraq in an honorable and strategic way as part of a larger process of rebuilding our standing in the world. We will have passed universal health care and not only expanded coverage, but started on the road toward a more efficient system. And we will have a bold energy agenda that drastically reduces our emission of greenhouse gases while creating a green engine that can drive growth for many years to come.[10]

On Foreign Policy

To renew American leadership in the world, as president, Barack said he would invest in common humanity and that a global engagement

> cannot be defined by what we are against, but that it must be guided by a clear sense of what we stand for. We have a significant stake in ensuring that those who live in fear and want today can live with

dignity and opportunity tomorrow ... to build a better, freer world, we must first behave in ways that reflect the decency and aspirations of the American people.[11]

In May 2007, Barack said that after a U.S. withdrawal pushes Iraqi leaders towards political accommodation, the new president should make a commitment to resolving the Israeli-Palestinian conflict, "a task that the Bush administration neglected for years." He called for a dialogue with Iran and Syria, noting, "our policy of issuing threats and relying on intermediaries ... is failing. Although we must not rule out using military force, we should not hesitate to talk directly." Barack said the Army should grow by 65,000 soldiers and the Marine Corps by 27,000 members. He said he would focus increased attention on Afghanistan and Pakistan, which he called "the central front in our war against al-Qaeda." Barack noted: "People around the world have heard a great deal of late about freedom on the march. Tragically, many have come to associate this with war, torture, and forcibly imposed regime change."[12]

> Throughout the Middle East, we must harness American power to reinvigorate American diplomacy. Tough-minded diplomacy, backed by a whole range of instruments of American power—political, economic, and military—could bring success even when dealing with long-standing adversaries such as Iran and Syria. Our policy of issuing threats and relying on intermediaries to curb Iran's nuclear program, sponsorship of terrorism, and regional aggression is failing ... To renew American leadership in the world, we must confront the most urgent threat to the security of America and the world—the spread of nuclear weapons, material, and technology and the risk that a nuclear device will fall into the hands of terrorists ... As president, I will work with other nations to secure, destroy, and stop the spread of these weapons in order to dramatically reduce the nuclear dangers for our nation and the world. America must lead a global effort to secure all nuclear weapons and material at vulnerable sites within four years—the most effective way to prevent terrorists from acquiring a bomb.[13]

Senator Hillary Clinton suggested many times during the presidential campaign that Barack did not have the foreign policy experience required to be president and suggested he had less foreign policy experience than any president since World War II. Barack responded to the charge in December 2007:

> They want to press what they consider to be a comparative advantage. It seems to get less traction as people hear me talk. If Senator Clinton has specific differences with me on Iraq, Iran, Burma, she can pick her hot spot, and we'll have a fruitful debate. The American people might not agree with everything I say, but I don't think they'll say, "The guy doesn't know what he's talking about."[14]

Keith Reinhard of the advertising agency DDB Worldwide also started a business in 2002 called Business for Diplomatic Action, a coalition of marketing, political science, and media professionals aimed at improving the standing of America in the world through business outreach. After commissioning research and testifying before Congress, Reinhard distilled his advice to one word: Listen. "Everywhere I go, from CEOs to people on the street, I hear the same thing. The U.S. needs to listen to the world." Author Ellen McGirt, in her article entitled "The Brand Called Obama," which appeared in the magazine *Fast Company* in April 2008, said,

> This is precisely the strategy that Obama professes in international relations: to engage, even with countries that have been viewed as America's enemies ... Obama's strategy is not one that all geopolitical experts agree with, but it is consistent with his criticism at home of what he terms "a politics that says it's okay to demonize your political opponents when we should be coming together to solve problems."

McGirt writes, "Obama's candidacy and its call for change may already be resonating in countries that have lamented U.S. policy but still want to believe in the promise of American leadership." "That Obama exists has already begun to recalibrate the way the world sees us. This is a good thing," says Keith Reinhard.[15]

On his foreign policy experience, Barack has noted that "experience in Washington is not knowledge of the world" and speaks to his upbringing where he lived and traveled in foreign countries and also to his work on the Senate Foreign Relations Committee. He also noted that foreign policy experience is often not gained by visiting a country's airport and embassy and then leaving. Barack's foreign policy positions represent fundamental philosophical differences with Senator John McCain, the Republican party's nominee for president in 2008. According to Susan E. Rice, a former assistant secretary of state for African affairs, a National Security Council official, and one of Barack's foreign policy advisors, Barack's experience can "provide a different kind of insight than the traditional resume," adding:

> At a time when our foreign policy and national security have so obviously suffered from a simplistic, black-and-white interpretation, an American president who spent part of his formative years and young adulthood living in a poor country under a dictatorship [Indonesia] brings an understanding of the complexity of things that others may not have. I'm not saying that official travels and Congressional delegations are without value, but there are limits to what you can glean from that.[16]

In April 2008, General David Petraeus and the Ambassador to Iraq, Ryan Crocker, spoke at their semiannual hearings before Congress. At the hearing, Barack asked both Petraeus and Crocker about "two main threats: Sunni terrorists like al-Qaeda in Iraq, and Iran." He noted that al-Qaeda had been rejected by the Iraqi Sunnis and chased to the northern city of Mosul. If, he asked, U.S. and Iraqi troops succeeded there, what was next? He proposed, "Our goal is not to hunt down and eliminate every single trace of al-Qaeda but rather to create a manageable situation where they're not posing a threat to Iraq." Petraeus said that Barack was "exactly right." When Barack asked Crocker about Iran: "We couldn't expect Iran to have no influence in Iraq, could we?" Crocker replied, "We have no problem with a good, constructive relationship between Iran and Iraq. The problem is with the Iranian strategy of backing extremist militia groups and sending in weapons and munitions that are used against Iraqis and against our own forces." Barack asked, "If Iran is such a threat to Iraq, why was Iranian President Mahmoud Ahmadinejad greeted with open arms and apparently a lot of official kissing in Baghdad last month?" Crocker replied, "A visit like that should be in the category of a normal relationship." Barack then noted that the current situation in Iraq was "messy," and that "There's still violence; there's still some traces of al-Qaeda; Iran has influence more than we would like. But if we had the current status quo and yet our troops had been drawn down to 30,000, would we consider that a success?"[17]

In an interview with Richard Wolffe of *Newsweek* in April 2008, Barack spoke about his trip to Pakistan in the early 1980s to stay with a college friend and how his early travels have shaped his views on foreign policy. Wolffe asked Barack what stuck with him about his time in Pakistan. Barack replied, "You had at that time a military government, you had a lot of problems with corruption, a lot of unemployed young men on the streets, a very wealthy ruling class ... there were a lot of trends that were similar to what I saw in Indonesia and what I would later see in Kenya." When asked if his experiences inform his approach to Pakistan today, Barack said,

> What it tells me is that the most important aspect of our foreign policy is not simply our relations with the rulers of these countries, but also our appreciation and understanding of the challenges and hardships and the struggles that ordinary people are going through ... without understanding that our choice in a place like Pakistan is not simply [between] military dictatorship or Islamic rule, led us to make a series of miscalculations that has weakened our fight against terrorism.

In response to a global summit of Muslim leaders early in his presidency, Barack replied,

> I think that I can speak credibly to them about the fact that I respect their culture, that I understand their religion, that I have lived in a Muslim country, and as a consequence I know it is possible to reconcile Islam with modernity and respect for human rights and a rejection of violence.

Barack said he was the "anti-doctrine candidate," and did not believe in abstractions when it comes to foreign policy; that decisions must be made based on an understanding of America's power and limits, and an understanding of history. Barack said that the single most important national security threat that America faces is on nuclear weapons, and that if nuclear weapons are kept out of the hands of terrorists, America can then handle the terrorists. This, he stated, would be one of his highest priorities as president.[18]

On the Economy

In April 2008, Maria Bartiromo, the anchor of the CNBC network program "Closing Bell with Maria Bartiromo," interviewed Barack for *Business Week Online*. She asked Barack, "Why raise taxes in a slowdown? Isn't that going to put a further strain on people?" Barack responded,

> There's no doubt that anything I do is going to be premised on what the economic situation is when I take office next January. The thing you can be assured of is that I'm not going to make these decisions based on ideology ... but I believe in the market. I believe in entrepreneurship. I believe in capitalism, and I want to do what works. One of the problems of the Bush Administration has been its rigidness when it comes to economic policy. It doesn't matter what the problem is, they'll say tax cuts ... At a certain point, if you've only got one arrow in the quiver, you're going to have problems.[19]

In an interview with the *Scranton Times-Tribune*, in Scranton, Pennsylvania on April 21, 2008, Barack was asked if there was only one thing he could accomplish to improve the economy, what it would be. Barack answered,

> It would be to invest in clean energy, to lower demand and lower gas prices and create millions of jobs in clean and renewable energies like win and solar and biodiesel. I think that would make a huge improvement—long term ... short term, our most urgent need is stabilizing our housing market ... I propose to get borrowers and lenders to work together to set up fixed interest rate mortgages ... that will in turn stabilize the financial market and get credit going again so we can pull out of this recession as quickly as possible.[20]

On Health Care

In a speech in Iowa City, Iowa on May 29, 2007, Barack spoke about health care and what he calls his "Plan for a Healthy America."

> We now face an opportunity—and an obligation—to turn the page on the failed politics of yesterday's health care debates. My plan

begins by covering every American. If you already have health insurance, the only thing that will change for you under this plan is the amount of money you will spend on premiums. That will be less. If you are one of the 45 million Americans who don't have health insurance, you will have it after this plan becomes law. No one will be turned away because of a preexisting condition or illness.

Barack said to the Iowa crowd, "We have reached a point in this country where the rising cost of health care has put too many families and businesses on a collision course with financial ruin and left too many without coverage at all."[21] To pay for the plan, Barack proposed restoring the tax rates for the "wealthiest" individuals back to the levels during the Clinton administration.

In April 2007, prior to the Iowa speech, the Democratic candidates held a forum on health care in Las Vegas. *The Economist* editorialized on Senator Clinton's seeming mastery of the subject of universal health coverage, and on how Barack "resorted to empty waffle, endorsing the idea of universal coverage but confessing that he had not yet produced a health care plan. An odd failure, given that the forum was devoted to the subject—and that this is one of the most important issues for Democratic voters." Replying to this editorial charge, Barack and his campaign team quickly stated that a plan was in the works.[22] The comparisons of Senator Clinton and her positions on the issues important to Americans to Barack and his positions began prior to Barack becoming a candidate and continued throughout the long 2008 campaign.

David Sirota, writing for *The Nation*, interviewed Barack in his office in Washington, D.C. Sirota asked Barack about what kind of leadership progressives can expect from him. Barack said,

> I am agnostic in terms of the models that solve problems. If the only way to solve a problem is structural, institutional change, then I will be for structural, institutional change. If I think we can achieve those same goals within the existing institutions, then I am going to try do that, because I think it's going to be easier to do and less disruptive and less costly and less painful ... I think everybody in this country should have basic health care. And what I'm trying to figure out is how to get from here to there.

Barack went on to tell Sirota about his support for other structural changes, including public financing of elections, strong labor protections to trade pacts, and efforts to create a more just tax system. He later decided, in June 2008, against accepting public financing for his election bid.[23]

Speaking at a health care forum in Las Vegas in 2007, Barack spoke about preventative care:

> We've got to put more money in prevention. It makes no sense for children to be going to the emergency room for treatable ailments like asthma. Twenty percent of our patients who have chronic illnesses account for eighty percent of the costs, so it's absolutely critical that we invest in managing those with chronic illnesses.

On health insurance, Barack said,

> We have to change the way we finance health care, and that's going to mean taking money away from people who make out really well right now ... the insurance companies make money by employing a lot of people to try to avoid insuring you and then, if you're insured, to try to avoid paying for the health care you received ... If you're starting from scratch, then a single-payer system would probably make sense. But we've got all these legacy systems in place, and managing the transition ... would be difficult to pull off. So we may need a system that's not so disruptive that people feel like suddenly what they've known for most of their lives is thrown by the wayside.[24]

In Iowa City, Barack offered a plan to provide health care to millions of Americans and more affordable medical insurance, financed in part by tax increases on the wealthy. He "bemoaned a health care cost crisis," calling it "unacceptable that 47 million in the country are uninsured while others are struggling to pay their medical bills." He said "the time is ripe for reforming the health care system despite an inability to do so in the past." Barack added, "We can do this. The climate is far different than it was the last time we tried this in the early nineties." Barack's first promise as a presidential candidate was that he would sign a universal health care plan into law by the end of his first term in the White House. There were disputes over whether his plan would provide universal care and that it aimed at lowering costs so all Americans can afford insurance but did not guarantee everyone would buy it. Ron Pollack, executive director of the advocacy group Families USA, praised Barack and other leading Democratic candidates for focusing on improving health care, but said of Barack's plan, "It's not totally clear that it would result in universal coverage." He added: "What makes it a top national priority now is not simply a sense of sympathy for people who are uninsured but a sense of fear that the coverage that used to be taken for granted can no longer be taken for granted." Barack's campaign stated that everyone would buy health insurance if it were affordable enough, achieving universal care. If some Americans were still uninsured after a few years into the plan, Barack would reconsider how to get to 100 percent.[25]

In an interview with *Newsweek* in February 2008, Barack was asked about the issues facing Americans today and what he would do as president. On health care, Barack answered,

> [T]he critical issue is the ability to mobilize the American people to move forward. The problem on health care is not the technical one—we all talk to the same experts. The question is who can build working majorities to push this stuff through. I don't think any fair-minded observer would suggest that Hillary Clinton is best equipped to break us out of the political gridlock that exists in Washington.[26]

On Education

Barack spoke to a group of students at Lincoln Land Community College in Springfield, Illinois in October 2004. He said, "We have an obligation and a responsibility to be investing in our students and our schools. We must make sure that people who have the grades, the desire and the will, but not the money, can still get the best education possible."[27]

In an interview for the journal *Black Issues in Higher Education* in October 2004, Barack was asked about personal responsibility and the need for greater commitment to and respect of academic excellence.

> We have to redouble our commitment to education within our own communities and within our homes, and raise the bar for our

children in terms of what we expect from them. It's not enough that they just graduate ... just believing that education is not only for our economic future, but it's also important just to give meaning to your life and give you a broader perspective on the world, that's something I think we have to recapture. And I say recapture because a generation ago I think there was greater respect for educational achievement within out communities.[28]

On the question of inner-city poverty and dysfunction, Barack proposed early childhood education, afterschool and mentoring programs, and efforts to teach young parents how to be parents. He also emphasized personal responsibility:

The framework that tends to be set up in Washington—which is either the problem is not enough money and not enough government programs, or the problem is a culture of poverty and not enough emphasis on traditional values—presents a false choice. There is a strong values-and-character component to educational achievement. To deny that is to deny reality, and I don't want to cede that reality to conservatives who use it as an excuse to underfund the schools ... Sometimes people think that when we talk about values, that somehow that's making "lift yourself up by your own bootstraps" argument and letting the larger society off the hook. That's why I always emphasize that we need both individual responsibility and mutual responsibility ... if a child is raised in a disorderly environment with inadequate health care and guns going off late at night, then it's a lot harder to incorporate those values. We as a society can take responsibility for creating conditions in which those cultural attributes are enhanced.[29]

In June 2007, Barack attended the National Education Association meeting and told the crowd that he's "committed to fixing and improving our public schools instead of abandoning them and passing out vouchers." He said that Washington "left common sense behind when they passed No Child Left Behind," and that teacher pay must be raised "across the board." He told the teachers, "If you excel at helping your students achieve success, your success will be valued and rewarded as well." He added that this must be done "with teachers, not imposed on them, and not based on some arbitrary test score."[30]

Senator Clinton won the New Hampshire Primary on January 8, 2008. In his speech that night, Barack spoke about the primary and the issues of the day. On education, Barack told the crowd of supporters,

> We can stop sending our children to schools with corridors of shame and start putting them on a pathway to success. We can stop talking about how great teachers are and start rewarding them for their greatness. We can do this with our new great majority.[31]

To many, affirmative action suggests that all African Americans come from poverty and always face discrimination when applying to the nation's colleges and universities. Barack has suggested that his two daughters should not benefit from affirmative action because of their privileged upbringing. On this issue and how it is used in higher education, Barack said the following in April 2008:

> I think that the basic principle that should guide discussions not just of affirmative action, but how we are admitting young people to college generally, is how do we make sure that we're providing ladders of opportunity for people? How do we make sure that every child in America has a decent shot in pursuing their dreams? I still believe in affirmative action as a means of overcoming both historic and potentially current discrimination, but I think it can't be a quota system and it can't be something that is simply applied without looking at the whole person, whether that person is black, or white, or Hispanic, male or female. What we want to do is make sure that people who've been locked out of opportunity are going to be able to walk through those doors of opportunity in the future.[32]

When the Democratic primary moved to Indiana in May 2008, polls showed that the race was extremely close. Both Barack and Clinton dispatched their spouses to campaign. Michelle Obama spoke about education: "Let's not elect somebody who has been there and hasn't done it," she said, adding that education was the issue that most concerns parents and that her husband was the only one who could make changes in education.

> It's going to take us being, as a nation, deeply passionate and angry about the failing education for all kids. When was the last time we

had some really solid questions for these candidates on education in a debate? You know all about the issues in our personal lives, but ... education is the thing we should be angry about.[33]

On Energy and the Environment

At a League of Conservation rally for John Kerry, the Democratic candidate for the presidency in 2004, Barack made a speech that brought environmental activists to their feet. He said,

> Environmentalism is not an upper-income issue, it's not a white issue, it's not a black issue, it's not a South or a North or an East or a West issue. It's an issue that all of us have a stake in. And if I can do anything to make sure that not just my daughter but every child in America has green pastures to run in and clean air to breathe and clean water to swim in, then that is something I'm going to work my hardest to make happen.[34]

After getting his law degree from Harvard, Barack became a civil-rights lawyer. When elected to the Illinois state senate in 1996, he distinguished himself as a leader on environmental and public health issues. In 2003, Barack was one of six state senators to receive a 100% environmental voting record award from the Illinois Environmental Council.[35]

On April 3, 2006, Barack spoke on the Senate floor regarding energy independence and about the planet. He said,

> For decades, we've been warned by legions of scientists and mountains of evidence that this was coming—that we couldn't just keep burning fossil fuels and contribute to the changing atmosphere without consequence. And yet, for decades, far too many have ignored the warnings, either dismissing the science as a hoax or believing that it was the concern of enviros looking to save polar bears and rainforests.[36]

Columnist Joe Klein reported from the campaign trail for *Time* magazine. On the energy issue, Barack said,

> When I call for increased fuel-economy standards, that doesn't sit very well with the [United Auto Workers], and they're big buddies of

mine ... Look, it's just not my style to go out of my way to offend people or be controversial just for the sake of being controversial. That's offensive and counterproductive. It makes people feel defensive and more resistant to changes.[37]

In June 2007, Barack spoke to the Detroit Economic Club. He asserted that any aid Washington gives automakers for their soaring health-care costs should be tied to improving fuel efficiency. He noted,

We anticipated that there weren't necessarily going to be a lot of applause lines in that speech. It was sort of an eat-your-spinach approach. But one thing I did say to people was that I wasn't going to make an environmental speech in California and then make a different speech in Detroit.[38]

Reviewing Barack's environmental record, author Amanda Griscom Little wrote in her article for Salon.com entitled "Obama on Energy for '08" that in his two and a half years in the U.S. Senate, Barack Obama has been active on matters of energy and the environment: "The Democrat from Illinois has introduced or co-sponsored nearly a hundred eco-related bills on issues ranging from lead poisoning and mercury emissions to auto fuel economy and biofuels promotion. Along the way, he has racked up a notable 96 percent rating from League of Conservation Voters." In this same article, Barack was asked how he would structure policies. Barack responded,

Through greater fuel economy and the use of hybrid and plug-in vehicles, we can notably reduce our dependence on foreign oil over the next decade. It is important to note that domestic fuel security, environmental protection and economy development all must be considered in unison as we progress ... so that as we move forward ... we do so responsibly.[39]

On the campaign trail in South Carolina, Barack was asked what he would do to lower gas prices. Barack answered,

I don't want to lie to you—there are not that many good short-term solutions. But the truth is, the primary problem we've got is we consume too much gas. Any politician who comes in and says he's going to be lowering gas prices right away is just not telling the truth.[40]

On Immigration

Barack has played a key role in supporting bipartisan efforts led by Senators John McCain and Edward Kennedy to legislate immigration reform. Barack's immigration platform centers on three concepts: border security, employer accountability, and earned citizenship.

> We have a right and a duty to protect our borders. We can insist to those already here that with citizenship come obligations—to a common language, common loyalties, a common purpose, a common destiny. But ultimately the dangers to our way of life is not that we will be overrun by those who do not look like us or do not yet speak our language ... if we withhold from them the rights and opportunities that we take for granted, and tolerate the hypocrisy of a servant class in our midst ... or if we stand idly by as America continues to become increasingly unequal, an inequality that tracks racial lines and therefore feeds racial strife and which, as the country becomes more black and brown, neither our democracy nor our economy can long withstand.[41]

On May 23, 2006, Barack spoke on the Senate floor regarding employment verification as part of the amendment for the Immigration Bill. He said,

> One of the central components of immigration reform is enforcement, and this bill contains a number of important provisions to beef up border security. But that's not enough. Real enforcement also means drying up the pool of jobs that encourages illegal immigration. And that can only happen if employers don't hire illegal workers.[42]

On the Constitution and Civil Rights

In mid-June 2007, a group of Iowans waited patiently to ask Barack questions. A high school student wearing a camouflage hat asked, "I'm a hunter and a competitive shooter. I wanna (sic) know your policy on firearms." Barack answered,

I believe that the Second Amendment means something. I believe that hunters and sportsmen should have the right to engage in those activities. I do believe in some commonsense gun-control laws. Stronger background checks ... I think we should be able to find a balance where you're able to do what you do and also not have random shootings all the time.[43]

On the issue of civil rights, Barack can claim to be part of a younger generation of activists. In March 2007, MSNBC commentator Tucker Carlson noted that Barack is not a product of the Civil Rights movement, saying, "he's a product of a much broader experience than that. Black politics will never be the same after his running for president." Author John K. Wilson, in his book *Barack Obama, The Improbable Quest* notes that Barack is not a "post-Civil Rights" politician, but rather he is a "because of Civil Rights" politician. Wilson writes that Barack is too young to have ever marched in the Civil Rights movement of the 1960s, but he has been directly involved in civil rights as a community organizer, helping blacks on the south side of Chicago in their fight for civil rights, and as a civil rights attorney and lecturer at the University of Chicago Law School. Furthermore, as a state legislator Barack worked to pass legislation to stop racial profiling by police and also worked on other civil rights matters during his years in Illinois state politics.[44] Donna Brazile, who was a part of Al Gore's campaign in 2000 and a Democratic strategist, said, "Now we have a politician that's coming to us, not from the Civil Rights chapter but the chapter that Martin Luther King wanted us to get to."

On May 24, 2006, Barack spoke on the Senate floor in opposition to the amendment requiring photo identification to vote. He said,

There is no more fundamental right accorded to United States citizens by the Constitution than the right to vote. The unimpeded exercise of this right is essential to the functioning of our democracy. Unfortunately, history has not been kind to certain citizens in protecting their ability to exercise this right.[45]

On the issue of civil unions and gay marriage, Barack said the following on June 5, 2006:

Today, we take up the valuable time of the U.S. Senate with a proposed amendment to our Constitution that has absolutely no chance of passing. We do this, allegedly, in an attempt to uphold the institution of marriage in this country. We do this despite the fact that for over two hundred years, Americans have been defining and defending marriage on the state and local level without any help from the U.S. Constitution at all.[46]

Barack added, "I agree with most Americans, with Democrats and Republicans, with Vice President Cheney, with over 2,000 religious leaders of all different beliefs, that decisions about marriage, as they always have, should be left to the states."[47]

On the Iraq War, the War on Terror, National Security, and America's Military

In October 2002, when a group of anti-war activists invited Barack to speak at an anti-war rally in Chicago, Barack's friends and supporters did not encourage his attendance. However, he decided he would speak. At the rally, held at Federal Plaza in downtown Chicago in front of a crowd of approximately 2,000 people, Barack took a position on what was, at the time, a war that most Americans supported. Barack said,

> What I am opposed to is a dumb war. What I am opposed to is a rash war ... what I am opposed to is the attempt ... to distract us from a rise in the uninsured, a rise in the poverty rate, a drop in the media income—to distract us from corporate scandals and a stock market that has just gone through the worst month since the Great Depression. That's what I'm opposed to. A dumb war. A rash war. A war based not on reason but on passion, not on principle but on politics.[48]

Barack told the crowd,

> I know that even a successful war against Iraq will require a U.S. occupation of undetermined length, at undetermined cost, with undetermined consequences. I know that an invasion of Iraq without a clear rationale and without strong international support will only fan the flames of the Middle East, and encourage the worst, rather

than best, impulses of the Arab world, and strengthen the require-
ment arm of al-Qaeda.[49]

Perhaps it was because Barack was a rather obscure Illinois state senator
in the midst of a re-election campaign that the Chicago anti-war rally
received little attention. However, after his speech at the Democratic
National Convention, as the media began to follow him everywhere, as
attention mounted about his run for the presidency, and after he
announced his bid for the presidency in February 2007, the anti-war
speech took on an unrivaled significance. It was described as powerful,
as fortuitous, and as it turned out, certainly timely. Barack could easily
say he was not in the Senate when the members voted to give President
Bush authorization for the Iraq war, and he could also say he was against
the war from the start. At the time of the speech, President Bush enjoyed
a very high approval rating, and polls showed that a majority of Americans were in favor of a war in Iraq. Barack had every reason to believe
that the war would continue to be popular and his opposition might
cause him to lose his future ambitions for national office. Still, he gave
the speech and continued his opposition to the Iraq war.

In November 2006, David Remnick interviewed Barack at the
American Magazine Conference in Phoenix, Arizona. Remnick asked
Barack what he felt were the worst instances of disaster by the Bush
Administration and where he disagreed the most with the Administra-
tion. Barack answered that it was foreign policy that was the most
obvious.

> I think the war in Iraq has been—was flawed ... and has done
> enormous damage to our standing around the world ... has
> weakened us in our capacity to deal with terrorism ... we have used
> so much political capital there that we have not been effective on
> issues like Iran, North Korea, Darfu ... it has gutted our military.[50]

Columnist Margaret Carlson of *Bloomberg News* wrote in January 2007
that Barack was (on Iraq) "dead-on correct about this seminal issue of
our time."[51]

The BBC News profiled Barack in January 2007. They described
him as "Rock star" and "beach babe," noting that these were not labels
normally applied to U.S. Senators. They quoted Barack's support of the
men and women serving in Iraq:

When we send our young men and women into harm's way, we have a solemn obligation not to fudge the numbers or shade the truth about why they're going, to care for their families while they're gone, to tend to the soldiers upon their return, and to never ever go to war without enough troops to win the war, secure the peace, and earn the respect of the world.[52]

The New Yorker compared the foreign policy stance of the Democrats running for president in January 2007. Barack told author Jeffrey Goldberg for the article,

It is not a great bargain for the next President to take over the mess in Iraq. But there is as much pressure in both the Republican and Democratic camps, because both have genuine concern for the troops and the families and the budget. It won't be good for congressmen of the President's party if we're still spending two billion dollars a week in Iraq in two years ... What I don't want to see happen is for Iraq to become an excuse for us to ignore misery or human rights violations or genocide ... We absolutely have an obligation to the Iraqi people. That's why I've resisted calls for an immediate withdrawal.[53]

Frank Rich, in his Sunday column for the *New York Times*, wrote about Barack and Barack's statement that he is "not interested in just splitting the difference" when he habitually seeks a consensus on tough issues. "There are some times where we need to be less bipartisan. I'm not interested in cheap bipartisanship. We should have been less bipartisan in asking tough questions about entering this Iraq war."[54]

In his announcement speech in February 2007, when he formally entered the presidential race, Barack told the crowd in Springfield, Illinois, "America, it's time to start bringing our troops home. It's time to admit that no amount of American lives can resolve the political disagreement that lies at the heart of someone else's civil war."[55]

When asked if senators who voted in favor of authorization bear some responsibility for the war in Iraq, Barack said, "The authorization allowed the administration to wage a war that has damaged national security ... I leave it up to those senators to make their own assessments in how they would do things differently or not."[56]

In an interview in February 2007, Barack said of the Iraq war,

The authorization vote is relevant only because it gives an insight into how people think about these problems and suggests the sort of judgment they apply in evaluation of a policy decision. There are people who sincerely believe that this was the best course of action, but in some cases politics entered into the calculation. In retrospect, a lot of people feel like they didn't ask hard enough questions.[57]

His opponents countered these statements with the fact that Barack had not given a policy speech on Iraq until he had been in the Senate for eleven months. In response, Barack stated that during his first year in the Senate, he took a deliberate low-key approach and did not make any major speeches on issues that were being discussed or voted upon, stating,

As a freshman, our objective was not to try to get in the front all the time. But the truth is that in that first year, we had just seen an Iraqi election, and my feeling was that while I was not optimistic, it was appropriate to try to give the nascent government a chance.[58]

At a rally in Atlanta, Georgia in April 2007, Barack ran through a litany of problems plaguing America and promised that the country could "make sure that every single American has health care in this country in the next six years, by the end of the next president's first term—by the end of my first term." He pledged to work towards a goal in which every car in the nation gets forty miles to the gallon and to revitalize the U.S. educational system, then added,

But we're not going to be able to even get started on some of these problems unless we bring an end to the senseless war in Iraq … It's about stubbornness and obstinacy. And we have to keep ratcheting up the pressure every day and every week to tell the President that it is time to change course, that it is time for us to start bringing our combat troops home from Iraq.[59]

Barack has adamantly stated that his position on the Iraq war was different than Senator Hillary Clinton's. On May 18, 2007, President Bill Clinton said the following of Barack's stance on the Iraq war: "This dichotomy that's been set up to allow him to become the raging hero of the anti-war crowd on the Internet is just factually inaccurate." Barack responded,

Well, I suppose that's true if you leave out the fact that she [Senator Hillary Clinton] authorized it and supported it, and I said it was a bad idea. You know, that's a fairly major difference … I think very highly of Senator Clinton. I think she is a wonderful senator from New York, but—and I think very highly of Bill Clinton. But I think that it is fair to say that we had a fundamentally different opinion on the wisdom of this war. And I don't think we can revise history when it comes to that.[60]

In May 2007, Barack voted against a measure to pay for the Iraq war that set no timetable for withdrawing U.S. troops. John McCain, who became the Republican nominee for the 2008 presidential race, said after the vote, "I was very disappointed to see Senator Obama and Senator Clinton embrace the policy of surrender. This vote may win favor with MoveOn and liberal primary voters, but it's the equivalent of waving a white flag to al Qaeda." Eli Pariser, executive director of MoveOn.org, said in response to the vote,

[t]hat no member of Congress who voted for the bill could pretend to be an opponent of the war … Senators Obama, Clinton and Dodd stood up and did the right thing—voting down the President's war policy. They're showing real leadership toward ending the war, and MoveOn's members are grateful. This bold stand … won't soon be forgotten.

Barack said of his vote, "This vote is a choice between validating the same failed policy in Iraq that has cost us so many lives and demanding a new one. And I am demanding a new one."[61]

Barack wrote in the July/August 2007 issue of the journal *Foreign Affairs*,

To renew American leadership in the world, we must first bring the Iraq war to a responsible end and refocus our attention on the broader Middle East … we must launch a comprehensive regional and international diplomatic initiative to help broker an end to the civil war in Iraq, prevent its spread, and limit the suffering of the Iraqi people … To renew American leadership in the world, we must immediately begin working to revitalize our military … rebuild and prepare it for the missions of the future … Enhancing our military will not be enough ... I would use our armed forces wisely ... I will clearly define the mission, seek out the advice of our military commanders, objectively evaluate intelligence, and ensure that our troops have the resources and the support they need. I will not hesitate to use force, unilaterally if necessary, to protect the American people or our vital interests whenever we are attacked or imminently threatened.[62]

As the fifth anniversary of the beginning of the Iraq war approached, Barack spoke at DePaul University. He said,

This is not just a matter of debating the past. It's about who has the best judgment to make the critical decisions of the future. This election is about ending the Iraq War, but even more it's about moving beyond it. And we're not going to be safe in a world of unconventional threats with the same old conventional thinking that got us into Iraq.

Barack proposed setting a goal of eliminating all nuclear weapons in the world, saying America should greatly reduce its stockpiles to lower the threat of nuclear terrorism. He added, "We will not pursue unilateral disarmament ... the best way to keep America safe is not to threaten terrorists with nuclear weapons. It's to keep nuclear weapons and nuclear materials away from terrorists."[63]

Senator Clinton won the New Hampshire Primary on January 8, 2008. In his concession speech that night, Barack spoke about the primary and the issues of the day. On Iraq, he said,

And when I am President, we will end this war in Iraq and bring our troops home; we will finish the job against al-Qaeda in Afghanistan; we will care for our veterans; we will restore our moral standing in the world; and we will never use 9/11 as a way to scare up votes, because it is not a tactic to win an election, it is a challenge that should unite America and the world against the common threats of the twenty-first century: terrorism and nuclear weapons; climate change and poverty; genocide and disease.[64]

In February 2006, Barack spoke on the Senate floor about energy security and its relation to national security. He said,

[E]very single hour we spend $18 million on foreign oil. It doesn't matter if these countries are budding democracies, despotic regimes, or havens for the madrassas that plant the seeds of terror in young minds—they get our money because we need their oil. One need only glance at headlines around the world to understand how dangerous this addictive arrangement truly is.[65]

NOTES

1. Barack Obama, "Renewing American Leadership," *Foreign Affairs,* July/August 2007.
2. Karen E. Crummy, "Obama: "The Country Calls Us," *Denver Post,* March 19, 2007, 1b.
3. Ibid.
4. Jim Spencer, "Obama Needs Inspiration to Get His Optimism Across," *Denver Post,* March 19, 2007.
5. Marc Royse, "Oprah Talks to Barack Obama," *O, the Oprah Magazine,* November 2004, 248.
6. David Sirota, "Mr. Obama Goes to Washington," *The Nation,* June 26, 2006, http://www.thenation.com (accessed May 23, 2008).
7. David Remnick, "Testing the Waters," *New Yorker,* November 6, 2006, http://www.newyorker.com (accessed May 23, 2008).
8. Jennifer Hunter, "Obama Brushes Off Race Question," *Chicago Sun Times,* December 2, 2007, http://www.suntimes.com (accessed December 7, 2007).
9. "Day 2 of 'Oprahpalooza' begins in SC," *Associated Press,* December 9, 2007, http://www.msnbc.msn.com (accessed December 10, 2007).
10. Jonathan Alter, "Obama Plays Offense," *Newsweek,* February 4, 2008, 32.
11. Barack Obama, "Renewing American Leadership," *Foreign Affairs,* July/August 2007.
12. Karen DeYoung, "Obama and Romney Lay Out Positions on Iraq and Beyond," *Washington Post,* May 31, 2007, A10.
13. Obama, "Renewing American Leadership."
14. Karen Tumulty, "Obama Finds His Moment," *Time,* December 10, 2007, 41.
15. Ellen McGirt, "The Brand Called Obama," *Fast Company,* April 2008, 92.
16. Larry Rohter, "Obama Says Real-Life Experience Trumps Rivals' Foreign Policy Credits," *New York Times,* April 10, 2008, http://www.nytimes.com (accessed April 10, 2008).
17. Joe Klein, "Petraeus Meets His Match," *Time,* April 21, 2008, 29.
18. Richard Wolffe, "America Can Be A Force (for) Good in the World," *Newsweek,* April 21, 2008, 24.
19. Maria Bartiromo, "Facetime with Barack Obama," *Business Week Online,* April 3, 2008, http://www.businessweek.com (accessed April 3, 2008).
20. Borys Krawczeniuk, "Interview with Barack Obama," *Scranton Times-Tribune,* April 21, 2008, http://www.timesshamrock.com (accessed April 21, 2008).

21. Barack Obama Web site, http://www.barackobama.com/issues/healthcare (accessed May 29, 2008).

22. "Where's the Beef?" *The Economist,* April 14, 2007, 36.

23. Sirota, "Mr. Obama Goes to Washington."

24. Larissa MacFarquhar, "The Conciliator," *New Yorker,* May 7, 2007, http://www. newyorker.com (accessed December 18, 2007).

25. "Obama Would Tax Wealthy to Pay for Universal Health Care," *CNN,* May 30, 2007, http://cnn.worldnews (accessed May 30, 2007).

26. Alter, "Obama Plays Offense."

27. Ronald Roach, "Obama Rising," *Black Issues in Higher Education,* October 7, 2004, 20–23.

28. Ibid.

29. Eugene Robinson, "The Moment for This Messenger?" *Washington Post,* March 13, 2007, A17.

30. Ruth Marcus, "From Barack Obama, Two Dangerous Words," *Washington Post,* July 11, 2007, A15.

31. Barack Obama, "Remarks: New Hampshire Primary," January 8, 2008, http:// thepage.time.com (accessed January 9, 2008).

32. Peter S. Canellos, "On Affirmative Action, Obama Intriguing but Vague," *Boston Globe,* April 29, 2008, http://www.boston.com (accessed April 29, 2008).

33. Abdon M. Pallasch, "Democratic Primary: Obama Urges Parents to Limit Children's Video Game Time," *Chicago Sun Times,* May 1, 2008, http://www.suntimes. com (accessed May 1, 2008).

34. Amanda Griscom, "Muckraker," *Salon,* August 6, 2004, http://dir.salon.com/story/ opinion/feature/2004/08/06/muck_obama/print.html (accessed May 29, 2008).

35. Ibid.

36. "Remarks by Senator Barack Obama on Energy Independence and the Safety of Our Planet, Chicago, Illinois," April 3, 2006, http://obama.senate.gov/speech (accessed May 29, 2008).

37. Joe Klein, "The Fresh Face," *Time,* October 23, 2006, 44.

38. Karen Tumulty, "The Candor Candidate," *Time,* June 11, 2007, 33–34.

39. Amanda Griscom Little, "Obama on Energy for '08," *Salon,* August 27, 2007, http://www.salon.com (accessed May 29, 2008).

40. Ryan Lizza, "Above the Fray," *GQ,* September 2007, 335.

41. Margaret E. Dorsey and Miguel Diaz-Barriga, "Senator Barack Obama and Immigration Reform," *Journal of Black Studies,* July 18, 2007, http://jbs.sagepub.com/ cgi/content/abstract/38/1/90 (accessed July 31, 2007).

42. "Floor Statement by Senator Barack Obama Employment Verification Amendment for the Immigration Bill," May 23, 2006, http://obama.senate.gov/speech (accessed May 29, 2008).

43. Lizza, "Above the Fray," 409.

44. John K. Wilson, *Barack Obama, This Improbable Quest* (Boulder, CO: Paradigm Publishers, 2008), 70.

45. "Floor Statement of Senator Barack Obama on the Amendment Requiring a Photo ID to Vote," May 24, 2006, http://obama.senate.gov/speech (accessed May 29, 2008).

46. Floor statement of Senator Barack Obama on the Federal Marriage Amendment," June 5, 2006, http://obama.senate.gov/speech (accessed May 29, 2008).

47. Ibid.

48. Barack Obama Web site, "Obama '08," http://my.barackobama.com (accessed October 3, 2007).

49. Wikisource contributors, "Barack Obama's Iraq Speech," *Wikisource, The Free Library,* http://en.wikisource.org/w/index.php?title=Barack_Obama%27s_Iraq_Speech&oldid=626318 (accessed May 9, 2008).

50. Remnick, "Testing the Waters."

51. Margaret Carlson, "For Obama, It's Public Character That Counts," *Bloomberg News,* January 4, 2007, http://www.blooomberg.com (accessed January 4, 2007).

52. "Profile: Barack Obama," *BBC News,* January 12, 2007, http://news.bbc.co.uk (accessed January 12, 2007).

53. Jeffrey Goldberg, "The Starting Gate," *New Yorker,* January 15, 2007, http://www.newyorker.com (accessed May 23, 2008).

54. Frank Rich, "Stop Him Before He Gets More Experience," *New York Times,* February 11, 2007, 4.12.

55. Adam Nagourney and Jeff Zeleny, "Obama Formally Enters Presidential Race with Calls for Generational Change," *New York Times,* February 11, 2007, 22.

56. Dan Balz, "With Campaign Underway, Obama Now Must Show More than Potential," *Washington Post,* February 13, 2007, A09.

57. Jeff Zeleny, "As Candidate, Obama Carves Antiwar Stance," *New York Times,* February 26, 2007.

58. Ibid.

59. Tom Baxter and Saeed Ahemed, "20,000 Turn Out for Obama," *Atlanta Journal Constitution,* April 14, 2007, http://www.ajc.com (accessed April 15, 2007).

60. Patrick Healy, "Obama Disputes Claim of Sharing Clinton's Stance on War," *New York Times,* May 18, 2007, A22.

61. John Whitesides, "Obama, Clinton Side with Anti-War Democrats," *Yahoo News,* May 25, 2007, http://news.yahoo.com/s/nm/20070525 (accessed May 25, 2007).

62. Obama, "Renewing American Leadership."

63. Jeff Zeleny, "Obama Highlights His War Opposition," *New York Times,* October 2, 2007, http://www.nytimes.com (accessed October 2, 2007).

64. Obama, "Remarks: New Hampshire Primary."

65. "Remarks of Senator Barack Obama, Governor's Ethanol Coalition, Energy Security is National Security," February 28, 2006, http://obama.senate.gov/speech (accessed May 29, 2008).

CHAPTER 7

The Youth Vote in the 2008 Campaign

"It's not that ordinary people have forgotten how to dream. It's just that their leaders have forgotten how."[1]

Introduction

Barack and his Democratic rival in the 2008 presidential race, Senator Hillary Clinton, were the favored candidates of younger Americans, according to a poll conducted by *CBS News*, *The New York Times*, and *MTV*, in June 2007. The poll results suggested that 18% said they were enthusiastic about Barack, and 17% were enthusiastic about Hillary Clinton; this was more than the Republican candidates with a total of 8%. Of Republican primary voters, 8% were excited about Barack. The poll also suggested that nearly eight in ten younger Americans think their generation would have a lot or some impact on who the next president would be, and six in ten said they were paying a lot or some attention to the campaign. Of those polled, most said that the 2008 presidential election was *the* most important, or one of the most important, in their lifetime.[2]

Since 2004, one characteristic of the 18-to 24-year-old voters is that they are more committed to the electoral process and politics in general. In the 2004 election, and in the primaries and caucuses held for the 2008 election, young voters have turned out in great numbers. Throughout his political career, Barack has included younger voters in his campaigns and has been able to bring in a new generation of voters. In 1992, he led a movement in Chicago called Project Vote, which registered 150,000 new voters. In the 2008 campaign, Barack and his political team have motivated youth to volunteer and to vote like no other candidate in history. He has tapped into what matters to the young voters in America by utilizing the Internet and social networking sites. His appeal to the youth in America is just one phenomenon of his campaign.

Caroline Kennedy, who endorsed Barack and appeared at several campaign rallies with him, wrote an op-ed piece for the *New York Times* entitled, "A President Like My Father." She wrote, "Senator Obama is inspiring my children, my parents' grandchildren, with that sense of possibility."[3]

In *Time* magazine, Caroline Kennedy, referring to her three teenagers, wrote, "They were the first people who made me realize that Barack Obama is the President we need."[4]

According to PBS commentator Bill Moyers, "Obama represents a generational metaphor. He opens up new gates so that younger people can feel that there's opportunity for them, that they can come in with him and create new possibilities."[5]

In his speech announcing his intention of running for president in the 2008 election, Barack said, "Each and every time, a new generation has risen up and done what's needed to be done. Today we are called once more—and it is time for our generation to answer that call." In the speech, Barack used the word "generation" no fewer than 13 times. According to *The Nation* magazine, his campaign theme is "It's time for the old to move over and make way for the new."[6]

Roger Cohen, columnist for the *New York Times,* wrote a column on January 28, 2008 entitled "Obama's Youth-Driven Movement" and stated "something is stirring in the U.S.A ... a political campaign has become a movement with Barack Obama at its head." Cohen wrote about a twenty-five-year-old student at George Washington University, who jumped in his car and drove seven hours from Washington, D.C. to campaign for Barack. The man, who was both white and a Republican, said,

> It was his all-encompassing message that got to me. I feel uplifted by him ... I'm 25 and for my entire life a Bush or a Clinton has been in the executive office, either as a vice-president or president. The United States is not about dynasties.

Cohen also wrote about seven Harvard students who'd driven for sixteen hours to get out the vote for the candidate. One said, "I'm here because I believe Obama has a chance at greatness." Another Harvard student said,

> Clinton is what our country has been. She's not where we're going, which is more diverse, more global, with fewer expectations about what it means to be black or white. Obama gets this from his upbringing.[7]

A New Hampshire lawyer told the *Boston Globe* after an Obama event: "I just turned 30, and the only politics I've known have been divisive. I'm ready for a new kind of politics, and I hope he's the one who can deliver it."[8]

The February 11, 2008 cover story of *Time* was "Why Young Voters Care Again," and included a subtitle, "And Why Their Vote Matters." The magazine noted that although youth participation increased in the

2004 election, in the 2008 election, "There seems to a youthquake. Young people sense that they are coming of age at a time when leadership—and their role in choosing it—really matters." Barack has been the catalyst, the magazine says, and also the beneficiary of greater youth involvement.[9]

"I am a believer that change can happen," says Patricia Griffin, twenty-five, a student at St. Louis Community College. "So-called Washington experience has given us an unjustified war, an economy slipping, the dollar losing its value, health care impossible to afford. I'm telling my friends they can make a difference this time. They can vote."[10]

A Republican college student drove three hours to hear Barack speak in Iowa. She declared, "Barack's attitude is awesome ... Barack's the only Democrat I'd vote for."[11]

The Obama campaign created MyBo, their own social networking tool, through which supporters can organize themselves however they see fit. The network claims more than half a million members and more than 8,000 affinity groups; some are organized by state (Ohioans for Obama!!), some by profession (Texas Business Women for Obama), and others by "groove thing" (Soul Music Lovers for Obama). According to Joe Rospars, the campaign's twenty-six-year-old director of new media who served as one of Howard Dean's chief online organizers, "We put these tools online as a public utility. We said to our supporters, 'Have at it.'" According to Rospars, that allowed supporters to mobilize on their own, which they did in unprecedented numbers. Before long, the campaign transformed hundreds of thousands of online donors into street-level activists. Donna Brazile, Al Gore's campaign manager and a member of the Democratic National Committee, noted, "Obama didn't just take their money. He gave them seats at the table and allowed them to become players." Barack's campaign also hired Steve Hildebrand as a strategist. "Steve Hildebrand, in shaping the campaign strategy from the outset, saw that there was an amazing opportunity here with Barack and young people," said Hans Riemer, the campaign's youth-vote director. Riemer noted that turnout has been astonishing among young people and that the youth vote has at least doubled and often tripled previous records in a number of the primary and caucus contests. "When I arrived at the Obama campaign, there were 175 Students for Barack Obama chapters already inexistence." The chapters started on Facebook in 2006 before moving into a sophisticated grass-roots organization. "My responsibility was to nurture it and work with them on their political strategy."[12]

In March 2008, Barack was endorsed by Senator Bob Casey of Pennsylvania in advance of the April 22, 2008 Democratic primary. Senator Casey decided to endorse Barack because of his "ability to bring disparate groups together and transcend some of these racial and other kinds of divides." Casey also noted that his four daughters were Barack supporters and were on his case to support him, too. Not that they dictated to him, he said, but he was paying attention. He wondered why are these kids, who are not very political, so interested? Casey said, "He [Barack] does have the ability to light up a younger generation."[13]

In an article entitled "The Brand Called Obama," which appeared in the April 2008 edition of *Fast Company* magazine, Keith Reinhard, chairman emeritus of DDB Worldwide, noted, "Barack Obama is three things you want in a brand. New, different, and attractive. That's as good as it gets." The article notes that Barack has his greatest strength among the young, roughly eighteen to twenty-nine years old, that advertisers covet, the cohort known as millennials—who will outnumber the baby boomers by 2010. What they share—new media, online social networks—is one place the Obama campaign has excelled. Barack deftly embraced and has been embraced by the Internet and has "been exceptionally successful at converting online clicks into real-world currency: rallies in the heartland, videos on YouTube, and most important, donations and votes." The campaign's website is "far more dynamic than any of the others and features constant updates, videos, photos, ringtones, widgets, and events to give supporters a reason to come back to the site." According to Andrew Rasieg, founder of the Personal Democracy Forum, a website that explores how technology is changing politics, "This is where the Obama campaign has been strategic and smart. They've made sure the message machine was providing the message where people were already assembled. They've turned themselves into a media organization."[14]

On May 25, 2008, Barack spoke at the Wesleyan University's Commencement, replacing Senator Edward Kennedy who had fallen ill. In his address to the graduating class, their families and friends, Barack talked about national service and said,

> I ask you to seek these opportunities when you leave here, because the future of this country—your future—depends on it. At a time

when our security and moral standing depend on winning hearts and minds in the forgotten corners of this world, we need more of you to serve abroad. As President, I intend to grow the Foreign Service, double the Peace Corps over the next few years, and engage the young people of other nations in similar programs, so that we work side by side to take on the common challenges that confront all humanity ... I am asking you, and if I should have the honor of serving this nation as President, I will be asking you again in the coming years. We may disagree on certain issues and positions, but I believe we can be unified in service to a greater good. I intend to make it a cause of my presidency, and I believe with all my heart that this generation is ready, and eager, and up to the challenge.[15]

NOTES

1. Lisa Rogak, ed., *Barack Obama, In His Own Words* (New York: Carroll & Graf Publishers, 2007), 49.
2. "Young Voters Favor Obama, Clinton," *CBS News,* June 26, 2007, http://www.cbsnews.com (accessed June 26, 2007).
3. Caroline Kennedy, "A President Like My Father," *New York Times,* January 27, 2008, WK.18.
4. David Von Drehle, "It's Their Turn Now," *Time,* February 11, 2008, 36.
5. John K. Wilson, *Barack Obama: This Improbable Quest* (Boulder, CO: Paradigm Publishers, 2008), 11.
6. Lakshmi Chaudhry, "Will the Real Generation Obama Please Stand Up?" *The Nation,* November 15, 2007, http://news.yahoo.com/s/thenation (accessed November 16, 2007). Article appeared in the December 3, 2007 edition of *The Nation.*
7. Roger Cohen, "Obama's Youth-Drive Movement," *New York Times,* January 28, 2008, http://www.nytimes.com (accessed January 28, 2008).
8. Wilson, *Obama: This Improbable Quest,* 13.
9. Richard Stengel, "Democracy Reborn," *Time,* February 11, 2008, 6.
10. Von Drehle, "It's Their Turn Now," 48.
11. Wilson, *Obama: This Improbable Quest,* 13.
12. Tim Dickinson, "The Machinery of Hope," *Rolling Stone,* March 20, 2008, 38.
13. Katherine Q. Seelye, "The Casey Endorsement," *New York Times,* March 28, 2008, http://www.nytimes.com (accessed March 28, 2008).
14. Ellen McGirt, "The Brand Called Obama," *Fast Company,* April 2008, 87–88.
15. Barack Obama, "Transcript of Obama's Wesleyan Commencement Address," *WFSB.com.* May 25, 2008, http://www.wfsb.com (accessed May 25, 2008).

CHAPTER 8

On Race and Faith

"I am comfortable in my own skin."[1]

"I am rooted in the African-American community. But I'm not limited by it."[2]

"As a teen, I had this divided identity—one inside the home, one for the outside world. It wasn't until I got to college that I started realizing that was fundamentally dishonest. I knew there had to be a different way for me to understand myself as a black man and yet not reject the love and values given to me by my mother and her parents. I had to reconcile that I could be proud of my African-American heritage and yet not be limited by it."[3]

"I feel confident that if you put me in a room with anybody—black, white, Hispanic, Republican, Democrat—give me half an hour and I will walk out with the votes of most of the folks. I don't feel constrained by race, geography, or background in terms of making a connection with people."[4]

"We need to take faith seriously not simply to block the religious right but to engage all persons of faith in the larger project of American renewal."[5]

Introduction

In the article "The Great Black Hope" in the November 2004 issue of *Washington Monthly*, editor Benjamin Wallace-Wells wrote that it is often said America is not ready for a black president. He wrote that it is true that most of today's most prominent African American politicians would have a hard time winning large numbers of white votes, both because of lingering racial resentments and a sense among whites that black politicians do not necessarily share their values and interests. Yet, Wallace-Wells writes, there are a few black politicians for whom their race is not a ball-and-chain, but instead, a jet engine, that launches them into stardom. For a small group of politicians, race has been an advantage because whites see in them confirmation that America, finally, is working. Author Wallace-Wells continues to say that to require politicians to transcend both race and ideology is an almost impossible standard, and one that white politicians need not meet at all. A prominent Virginia Democratic fundraiser was quoted in the article: "As wonderful as Barack is, the one thing you wonder is if we haven't made him out to be something more than it's possible for him to be. So much is expected of him." When America looked at Barack, Wallace-Wells notes, they saw a political character that they'd never quite encountered before. He was black, but not quite. He spoke white, with the hand-gestures of a management consultant, but also used the oratorical flourishes of a black preacher. In the speech at the Democratic National Convention, the author notes that Barack made himself as hard to peg politically as he had been racially, casting himself as a politician who did not proffer typically liberal solutions to cultural problems. He notes that Barack said in the speech that "Parents have to teach, that children can't achieve unless we raise their expectations and turn off the televisions sets and eradicate the slander that says a black youth with a book is acting white." Barack closed the address, "There's not a liberal America and a conservative America … a black America and a white America and Latino America and Asian America; there's the United States of America. The pundits like to slice and dice our country into red states and blue states … But I've got news for them, too. We worship an awesome God in the blue states, and we don't like federal agents poking around our libraries in the red states." Author

Wallace-Wells wrote that the pressure would be on Barack from the moment he is sworn in as a senator, that he will be in a position like none of his colleagues. His every move would be scanned for signs that he is preparing for a presidential run and that even among his most passionate supporters, there's a concern that before he runs, he should learn to walk. There is an emerging market for a certain kind of black president, he writes, the fulfillment of which will be both harder, and potentially more powerful, than any we have seen before, and that the chances are, somewhere in America, there is a person watching Barack's career carefully, and dreaming.[6]

On Race

> We as a black community are struggling with our own identity and what it means to be black. We see what is shown of us on TV but we also know that is not the full picture. So what is the picture? We're figuring it out. It's a conversation that needs to take place.
>
> Michelle Obama, in response to the persistent questions about Barack's roots[7]

> Nobody tells the story of the American dream better than Obama.
>
> David Ignatius, columnist, *Washington Post*[8]

> The secret to Martin Luther King was that he flattered white Americans that you are better than you think you are. The very essence of Obama's appeal is the idea that he represents racial idealism—the idea that race is something that America can transcend. That's a very appealing idea. A lot of Americans would truly love to find a black candidate they could comfortably vote for President of the United States.
>
> Shelby Steele, Stanford University's Hoover Institution[9]

Although Barack has said that he settled his own struggle with racial identity in his late teens and the questions about his authenticity were not new to him, he felt the debate over the issue of race was more about America's state of mind than it was about him and his candidacy. From his earliest days as a politician, Barack has made a career out of reconciling opposing sides. He's been able to assuage some conservative whites who have been surprised by his lack of grievance and encouraged by his pragmatism. And he has accomplished that, for the most part, without alienating African American supporters. As only the third African American ever to hold a seat in the U.S. Senate, Barack represents the emergence of a new generation of national political leaders. His keynote speech at the Democratic National Convention placed him in the national spotlight. Dr. Ronald Walters, a political scientist at the University of Maryland, wrote the following of Barack and the speech:

> He was put there to support the ticket, to hit the themes, and he did his job. And on that he got, I think, an accolade of a rising star and so forth. I tend to think that speech was one that tried to identify [Obama] as a non-racial politician that tried to connect with his immigrant roots, and tried to meet the theme of diversity that was thrust upon him. It was a theme that went over great with everybody in the convention—Blacks, Whites, everyone ... I would call him a liberal Democratic politician in terms of the kind of measures that he has supported—basic family-oriented measures, civil rights-oriented. To that extent, the profile of his agenda is very much compatible with the needs of the Black community.[10]

Sociologist Robert Lang, director of the Metropolitan Institute at Virginia Tech, stated that in America, barriers still exist, but they do not necessarily have the same meaning as even a decade ago, adding "Because people are exposed to different races, ethnicities and sexual orientations in their workplace, in their neighborhoods, in their communities, they are much more comfortable ... what used to make them raise their eyebrows now makes them shrug their shoulders."[11]

In his memoir *Dreams from My Father*, Barack wrote that it might have been because of growing up in Hawaii instead of on the more difficult streets and neighborhoods that left him without the feeling of needing to "escape." For him, there was nothing he had to escape except his own inner doubt. Over time, Barack succeeded in coming to terms with his race, with his absent father, and came to know clearly his ambitions and his calling. Still, when he announced his campaign for the presidency, the issue of racism in America bubbled up once again. At first, black voters appeared less than enthusiastic. One explanation was that African Americans did not believe Barack was representative of them, being the son of a Kenyan man and a white American woman. Many black voters were not eagerly or naturally gravitating to him as some may have first thought. There were some who were questioning his "blackness," asking if was he "black enough" to be their candidate. Barack is African and he is an American, but he is not an African American. Since his ancestors did not come to America on slave ships, this sets him apart from many blacks in America. In addition, some African Americans wondered if he was "real," if he could actually run a campaign and be taken seriously. It was only after winning the Iowa Caucus that many African Americans felt they could support Barack, that he was in fact real, and that by being accepted by voters in Iowa, voters all across America would look at him as a candidate that has something to say, and not viewed only as an African American candidate so different from all the other African Americans that had run for president before.

In his second book, *Audacity of Hope*, Barack wrote,

> To say that we are one people is not to suggest that race no longer matters—that the fight for equality has been won, or that the problems that minorities face in this country today are largely self-inflicted. We know the statistics ... to suggest that our racial attitudes play no part in these disparities is to turn a blind eye to both our history and our experience—and to relieve ourselves of the responsibility to make things right ... while my own upbringing hardly typifies the African-American experience ... I now occupy a position that insulates me from most of the bumps and bruises that the average black man must endure—I can recite the usual litany of petty slights that during my forty-five years have been directed my way: security guards tailing me as I shop in department stores, white couples who toss me their car keys as I stand outside a restaurant waiting for the valet, police cars pulling me over for no apparent reason. I know what it's like to have people tell me I can't do something because of my color, and I know the bitter swill of swallowed-back anger.[12]

When it was announced that Barack had been elected the president of the prestigious Harvard Law Review, the first African American to hold the spot in its 104-year history, he was inundated with newspaper and magazine reporters. In the interviews, he was modest in his responses and careful with his answers. In one interview, Barack said,

> The fact that I've been elected shows a lot of progress. It's encouraging. But it's important that stories like mine aren't used to say that everything is O.K. for blacks. You have to remember that for every one of me, there are hundreds or thousands of black students with at least equal talent who don't get a chance.[13]

Barack's first campaign was running for president of the *Harvard Law Review*. The voters were mostly white and at the time, the school was torn over racial issues including affirmative action. There was anger at the failure to appoint African American professors. There was also dismay at the influence of liberal scholars who condemned the criminal-justice system as skewed against minorities and the poor. Amid all of this, Barack was elected with the support of a block of conservative students. His former classmate Bradford Berenson, who later served in George W. Bush's White House, said, "What really set him apart from the people who had roughly the same views he did is that he did not demonize the people on the other side of the dispute. He was not the sort to accuse people of being racist for having different views of affirmative action."[14]

Many African Americans come from different backgrounds and the issue of blackness or a singular experience is difficult to explain or understand. Barack noted,

> My view has always been that I'm African-American. African-Americans by definition, we're a hybrid people. One of the things I loved about my mother was not only did she not feel rejected by me defining myself as an African-American, but she recognized that I was a black man in the United States and my experiences were going to be different than hers.[15]

In late April 2004, while campaigning for the U.S. Senate, Barack attended the Will/Grundy County Annual AFL-CIO Dinner to make a pitch for his candidacy. When Barack took the stage, he introduced himself as he often does, as the "skinny guy from the South Side," and noticeably moved the audience when he spoke about various issues.

Shortly after his speech, two middle-aged men, who identified them-selves as officials from the local branch of the American Federal of State, County and Municipal Employees, spoke about Barack's speech. The first man noted it was the first time he had seen Barack in person and that he especially liked the fact that Barack did not put anyone down, even Republicans. The second man said, "The thing about Obama is that there are no racial lines, there are no party lines. He reaches everybody." Author Noam Scheiber, who described the speech, also noted in his article that "The power of Obama's exotic background to neutralize race as an issue, combined with his elite education and his credential as the first African-American *Harvard Law Review* president, made him an African American candidate who was not stereotypically African-American." Pollster Mark Blumenthal said of Barack,

> [Obama] is not stereotypically anything. He's different. He's different because he's biracial. He's a different generation. He's different in terms of qualifications than nine of ten people who run for office.[16]

In November 2004, Barack appeared on the *Oprah Winfrey Show*. He was asked what he wanted to do with his politics. The first thing he said was, "I want to make real the American ideal that every child in this country has a shot at life." And the second and companion goal was:

> I'm well situated to help the country understand how we can both celebrate our diversity in all its complexity and still affirm our com-mon bonds. That will be the biggest challenge, not just for this country but for the entire planet. How do we say we're different yet the same? ... Of course, there will be times when we'll argue about our difference, but we have to build a society on the belief that you are more like me than different from me. That you know your fears, your hopes, your love for your child are the same as what I feel. Maybe I can help with that because I've got so many different pieces in me.[17]

In an interview with the *Chicago Tribune* in June 2005, Barack was asked what the most important racial issue is facing the country now. Barack responded, "Education. There is no denying that while individ-ual African-American students are doing wonderful and achieving at the highest levels, in the aggregate African-American students are still behind at every level." When asked about his own life experience and education being vastly different from the majority, Barack answered,

> I'm only one generation away from a parent who learned in a tin-roof shack in the backwoods of Kenya, not that different from a one-room, tin-roof schoolhouse in South Carolina or Mississippi ... Growing up I absorbed a lot of negative stereotypes about how I should behave as a black teenager and fell into some of the same traps that a lot of black male youth do. It wasn't preordained that I go to Columbia or to Harvard. I didn't have a father in the house, which meant that I didn't have a lot of role models in terms of how I should operate.

When asked if America was ready for a black president, Barack said, "Yes. I think an African-American candidate, if he's the best candidate, can be president."[18]

Jonathan Alter interviewed Barack in December 2006 for *Newsweek* magazine. Alter asked Barack about how crowds react to him, why he is striking such a chord in America, and whether this reaction is generational. Barack said that politics have been grounded in debates over the 1960s and the counter backlash within the Democratic Party against the 1960s. His peer group, Barack answered, finds that many of those divisions are unproductive and they see many problems differently, on race, faith, the economy, foreign policy, and the role of the military. Barack added,

> Part of the reason the next generation can see things differently is because of the battles that the previous generation fought. But the next generation is to some degree liberated from what I call the either/or arguments around these issues. So on race, the classic '60s formulation was, "is it society and institutional racism that's causing black poverty or is it black pathology and a culture of poverty?" And you couldn't choose "all of the above." It looks to me like both. [The younger generation] is much less caught up in these neatly packaged orthodoxies.[19]

Before Barack announced his candidacy for president, his appeal to blacks was an open question. Attending a luncheon in Chicago in January 2007, the Reverend B. Herbert Martin expressed both satisfaction and concern after listening to Barack speak. As the only black person in the otherwise white audience who applauded Barack's speech, the Reverend said he was thrilled that Barack could engender such enthusiasm from the audience because it offered further proof that he would be a formidable presidential candidate, but he also worried that in order to run successfully, Barack would have to become a different kind of politician than the one who earned the trust of voters on Chicago's mostly black south side as a state legislator before he was elected to the U.S. Senate in 2004. Martin said, "How does he identify himself? Will he continue to be an African-American, or will he become some of kind of new creation?" Melissa V. Harris-Lacewell, a Princeton University professor who followed Barack's rising political career, said that Barack may be forced to choose:

> You can be elected president as a black person only if you signal at some level that you are independent from black people. He is going to have to figure out whether there is a way not to alienate and anger a black base that almost by definition is going to be disappointed.

Reverend Martin asked,

> Who does he represent? That is what people are worried about. When you look and see who is surrounding him, you are not going to see too many brothers. What you see is the liberal left.[20]

On February 11, 2007, Barack appeared on CBS's *60 Minutes*. Interviewer Steve Kroft raised the issue that "there are African-Americans who don't think that you're black enough, who don't think that you have had the required experience." Barack answered:

> When I'm walking down the South Side of Chicago and visiting my barbershop and playing basketball in some of these neighborhoods, those aren't questions I get asked. I also notice when I'm catching a cab. Nobody's confused about that either ... If you look African-American in this society, you're treated as an African-American, and when you're a child, in particular, that is how you begin to identify yourself. It's interesting though, that now I feel very comfortable and confident in terms of who I am and where I stake my ground. But I notice that ... I've become a focal point for a racial debate.[21]

Secretary of State Condoleezza Rice found Barack "appealing" and said it would not be much longer before race was not a barrier to becoming president. As a top-tier contender among Democrats, his wide support in the 2008 race "just shows that we've come a very long way," she said in February 2007. Rice said that Barack is a member of the Senate Foreign Relations Committee, where she often testifies. She noted,

> I do think we've come a long way in overcoming stereotypes, role stereotypes about African-Americans. I will say race is still a factor. When a person walks into a room, I still think people still see race. I think he's very appealing and a great person. He's on my committee. And we've always had a good exchange. I think he's an extraordinary person.[22]

There was little doubt in anyone's mind that the 2008 race for the White House was historic; the race had the face of a changing America. The presidential field was filled with the kinds of candidates who would not have had a chance in years past, and polls conducted in early 2007 showed that voters were more open than ever before to groundbreakers. In 2008, the first woman ever may have been elected president; or it may have been the first Mormon, or the first black, the first Hispanic, the first Italian-American, the first thrice-married man, or the first person over 70. After 218 years and forty-two presidents, all white and male, the field of candidates included credible candidates whose race, gender, ethnicity, religion, or personal history probably would have ruled them out in the past. A *USA Today/Gallup* Poll found that only one in five Americans were "completely comfortable" with all of the breakthrough traits represented by the leading contenders in the 2008 field of candidates. Nearly one third had reservations about most of them. The poll found that women were no more likely than men to be comfortable voting for a woman; women over fifty were among the most skeptical of all. Blacks were no more likely than whites to be comfortable voting for a black. And seniors were less likely than the middle-aged to be comfortable voting for a seventy-two-year-old to become president. Steve Gillon, resident historian of The History Channel and a professor at the University of Oklahoma said,

> Presidential elections won't lead the way; they'll follow the change. In our presidential elections, we tend to elect figures who are reassuring.

The election of a woman president or an African-American president will be the last hurdle, not the first.[23]

In April 2007, Barack appeared at a meeting of black political organizers and said African Americans had been "complicit in diminishing ourselves," stating,

I've heard those words around the kitchen tables. All of us have been complicit in diminishing ourselves and engaging in the kind of self-hatred that keeps our young men and young women down. That's something we have to talk about in this election.

He added that he did not want the black vote simply because he was black, because that is not what America is about. "I want it to be because of what I've done, and how I've lived, and the principles I stand for, and the ideas I promote." Although this crowd of organizers warmly received him, the reception was not a rousing success.[24]

In May 2007, Barack received Secret Service protection, earlier than any other presidential candidate, excluding Senator Hillary Clinton, who received Secret Service protection as a former first lady. Concerns about his safety led to Barack receiving Secret Service detail. Senator Dick Durbin of Illinois said the early protection "had a lot to do with race. I wished we lived in a country where that is not a problem, but it still is. The fact that Barack Obama is such a highly visible African American candidate, I think increases his vulnerability." House Speaker Nancy Pelosi, Democrat from California, said, "I would just say this— the bipartisan leadership committee makes this decision, it didn't take long to decide that it would be important for Senator Obama to have this security." She did not share details, but added, "Suffice to say that it was self-evident that Senator Obama attracts a great deal of attention wherever he goes, so it was thought, under those circumstances, that he should have it." In response to the Secret Service detail on her husband, a spokesperson for Michelle Obama said, "The family is thankful for the protection and the peace of mind that the Secret Service is providing."[25]

Ron Walters, professor of government and politics at the University of Maryland, wrote in the *Journal of Black Studies* in July 2007 about Barack's universalistic perspective on policy issues. In an interview on National Public Radio in 2007, Barack said,

There has always been some tension between speaking in universal terms and speaking in very race-specific terms about the plight of the African-American community. By virtue of my background, I am more likely to speak in universal terms.

A contrasting view of Barack was noted from an interview with Representative Bobby Rush of Chicago (whom Barack ran against in his first unsuccessful bid for the U.S. House of Representatives), when Rush stated, "I'm a race politician and he's not. I don't compromise. I don't step back. I don't try to deny. I'm proud to be an African-American."[26]

When Steve Kroft of CBS News asked Barack in 2007 how important race was to his identity when he was growing up and at what point he decided he was black, Barack responded, "Well, I'm not sure I decided it. I think, you know, if you look African-American in this society, you're treated as an African-American ... that is how you identify yourself."[27]

Writing in the *American Prospect* magazine, author Terence Samuel stated,

[Obama] is in many ways the full flowering of a strain of up-tempo, non-grievance, American-Dream-In-Color politics. His counterparts are young, Ivy League professionals, heirs to the civil-rights movement who are determined to move beyond both the mood and the methods of their forebears.

Angela Davis, professor of history of consciousness at the University of California, Santa Cruz, wrote,

[Obama] is being consumed as the embodiment of color blindness. It's the notion that we have moved beyond racism by not taking race into account. That's what makes him conceivable as a presidential candidate. He's become the model of diversity in this period ... a model of diversity as the difference that makes no difference. The change that brings no change.[28]

The July 2007 *Newsweek* cover "Black and White," reported on whether Barack, as the nation's first black president, can appeal to both blacks and whites while still being true to himself, and stated that he faced many challenges in what he calls his "improbable candidacy." The magazine reported that few of the challenges Barack faced were as complex or as emotional as the politics of race. The cover article noted that on the day Barack announced his candidacy, Cornel West, the "brilliant and bombastic scholar" lambasted Barack's campaign. "He's got large numbers of white brothers and sisters who have fears and anxieties and concerns, and he's got to speak to them in such a way that he holds us at arm's length. So he's walking this tightrope." West, the magazine wrote, challenged the candidate to answer a stark set of questions:

> I want to know how deep is your love for the people, what kind of courage have you manifested in the stances that you have and what are you willing to sacrifice for. That's the fundamental question. I don't care what color you are. You see, you can't take black people for granted just 'cause you're black.

A few days later, the article noted, Barack called West in his Princeton office and the two men later met. A month after questioning the campaign, West endorsed Barack and signed up as an unpaid adviser. Barack told *Newsweek*,

> I think America is still caught in a little bit of a time warp: the narrative of black politics is still shaped by the '60s and black power. That is not, I think, how most black voters are thinking. I don't think that's how most white voters are think. I think that people are thinking about how to find a job, how to fill up the gas tank, how to send their kids to college. I find that when I talk about those issues, both blacks and whites respond well.

Newsweek reported that according to their latest poll, race was no longer the barrier it once was to electing a president. A clear majority— 59 percent—says the country is ready to elect an African American president, up from 37 percent at the start of the decade.[29]

By October 2007, almost 3 months prior to the beginning of the primary season and before the January 2008 Iowa Caucus, it seemed that Barack had just about everything going for him. The country was open to accepting a change in the political climate and Barack had a new message, a fresh face, and an inspirational message. He was raising money faster than any Democrat ever had, and from more people, including about 75,000 new donors. The question was why was his campaign not gaining ground. The race was historic, in gender and in race, but the race issue seemed to be more of a delicate challenge. Would black voters, the Democratic Party's most loyal constituency, vote for Barack, when traditionally they had an allegiance to the Clintons? The pollsters showed black voters as deeply divided, with Barack winning among younger and male African Americans and Hillary Clinton running stronger among older African American women. Pollsters also suggested that this could change if Barack's overall prospects improved. Barack continued to walk a fine line, demonstrating that he was connected to the African American community without appearing to have an agenda driven by only that constituency. Donna Brazile said,

> Race is not just an issue in the back of the minds of white voters. It really is a concern with black voters. They're worried about whether the country is ready for a black President. They're pessimistic ... He has the electability problem with black voters too.

Barack's advisors stated they were not worried and Barack sharpened his message with a new, edgier stump speech that included a harder message of change.[30]

In an October 2007 issue of *Essence* magazine, author and interviewer Gwen Ifill wrote an article about accompanying Barack on the campaign trail. Ifill wrote about Barack attracting 20,000 people in Austin, Texas and 15,000 in Oakland, California. In New Hampshire, Barack had attracted a smaller crowd, in a small town, on a Monday afternoon. Ifill notes in her article that the high voter engagement at nearly every stop suggests that voters are taking stock of Barack and she wonders if the appeal is due to familiarity or to race. Although Barack's biracial background may be appealing to some whites because he seems less black, some blacks could reject him because he seems white. Ifill cites a quote from Georgetown University professor Michael Eric Dyson, who calls Barack's dilemma the "pigment predicate." He notes, "At this level, race is trumping gender when it comes to the discomfort his candidacy might ultimately cause in the American citizenry. And I think Barack Obama is caught in the crosswinds of race." Ifill writes that Barack knows full well the tightrope he walks. Barack said,

> What I've tried to do is just say what I think and not worry about whether it's pleasing a particular audience or not. It is difficult because what I say oftentimes is read through a filter of racial experience. That can cause problems. But, you know, I've been straddling this line most of my life.

When asked if it is possible to get past this, Barack answered,

> I don't believe it is possible to transcend race in this country. Race is a factor in this society. The legacy of Jim Crow and slavery has not gone away. It is not an accident that African-Americans experience high crime rates, are poor, and have less wealth. It is a direct result of our racial history.

Ifill asked Barack directly if he really believed America was ready for a black president. Barack responded that he felt racial attitudes have changed sufficiently in this country, that people are willing to vote for him as president if they believe he can help them on health care, on education, and on the issues that are important in their lives. He added,

> Now, are there going to be people who don't vote for me because I am Black? Absolutely. But I do not believe those are people who would have voted for me, given my political philosophy, even if I were White.[31]

As Barack took his campaign across the country, telling his unique story of a white mother and a black father and how he has always lived between two worlds, he seemed to be tapping into a changed racial landscape among younger white people. Many said they were drawn to him and his message because they believed his mixed-race background reflected America's increasingly diverse population and projected a more optimistic vision of the country's racial future. Was his candidacy making a turning point in race and politics in America? In an article in *The Wall Street Journal* in November 2007, author Jonathan Kaufman wrote that whether Barack succeeded in winning the nomination or not, he was prompting significant numbers of white Americans to consider voting for him, despite his racial background, and perhaps because of it. A 24-year-old white social worker said, "Because he's black it makes me want to believe that he will change things. It feels like you are part of something that's starting to change American politics. It's the cool factor. He's a rock star." Bob Tuke, who is white and is the former chairman of the Tennessee Democratic Party, said, "Obama is running an emancipating campaign. He is emancipating white voters to vote for a black candidate." Sean Briscoe, a white 24-year-old, said, "Obama doesn't come with the baggage of the civil-rights movement, focusing entirely on the race issue. He went from Hawaii to Indonesia. He has been in all these places where you get an appreciation for people who aren't like you." Friends say that Barack's double life and heritage has affected not just his personality but also his politics. Mary Pattillo, an African American professor at Northwestern University who has known Barack for many years, said,

> Obama knows this is a majority white country. He is acutely aware how his discussion of race and racial politics will be interpreted and received by whites. We who work in the white world are always mindful of not making whites feel threatened. You can't get angry as a black person working in white America. To get a message across, black professionals are always thinking about the perfect balance of assertiveness and non-threateningness.

A *Wall Street Journal* poll published in the November 12, 2007 article noted that Barack's popularity among whites also stirred uneasiness among many blacks. At the time, he trailed Hillary Clinton among black voters by 9 percent.[32]

After the Maryland, Virginia, and Washington, D.C. primaries on February 12, 2008, Barack said the following in his victory speech:

> We have now won east and west, north and south, and across the heartland of this country we love. We have given young people a reason to believe, and brought folks back to the polls who want to believe again. And we are bringing together Democrats and Independents and Republicans; blacks and whites; Latinos and Asians; small states and big states; Red States and Blue States into a United States of America.[33]

Kenneth Walsh interviewed Barack for *U.S. News & World Report* and asked if in the end would race be an impediment to him being elected. Barack responded,

> I have no doubt that there are some people who won't vote for me because I'm black. There would also be some people who won't vote for me because I'm young, because I've got big ears … or they don't like my political philosophy. This country made profound changes after 1960 … essentially in my lifetime … changes in attitude. Now that is not to suggest that my election provides us racial reconciliation on the cheap. There are deep-rooted, institutional barriers to success for minority groups. Not just African-Americans but also Latinos. And those barriers—some of them cultural, some of the institutional—aren't going to go away anytime soon, unless we make some serious investments in improving our schools and opening up job opportunities and enforcing nondiscrimination laws more effectively than we have.[34]

Barack never asked African Americans to vote for him because he could become the first black president in U.S. history, but for many African Americans, the thought was exciting. Many felt his candidacy in terms of racial progress. In interviews people thought Barack's ability to win primary and caucus races in predominantly white states challenged a deep pessimism about the electoral prospects for an African American. Melissa Harris-Lacewell, professor of politics at Princeton University, said, "There is a population of African-Americans, specifically the masses of African-Americans … who see Barack Obama as the culmination of the civil rights movements and other movements against racial inequality. No one thought this would happen in our lifetime, or even in the lifetime of our children." After the win in the Iowa Caucus on January 3, 2008, where there were few black voters, Barack's popularity among South Carolina black voters began to soar, which suggested that his appeal in part was based upon his ability to rally a diverse constituency. William Jelani Cobb, a history professor at Spelman College in Atlanta, said,

> [Black] people want their vote to count. They may have thought that he was attractive as a candidate but they weren't going to vote for him if he had no chance. With Obama he is going for broke. That raised a higher bar for him getting support from black folk.

In a debate with Hillary Clinton in February 2008, Barack repeated a message central to his campaign, that he can help bring unity: "I can bring this country together I think in a unique way, across divisions of race, religion, region. And that is what's going to be required in order for us to actually deliver on the issues that both Senator Clinton and I care so much about."[35]

Barack asked voters to judge issues, not race. He expressed frustration that racial issues kept rising to the top of his presidential battle with Hillary Clinton, but he said the great majority of voters will base their decisions on substantive issues. At a news conference in Chicago in March 2008, Barack said he was not overly reliant on black support, but that he felt his primary victories in an array of states had proven that he could draw support from all races and regions. He said some voters might favor or disfavor him because he is black, just as some might favor or disfavor Clinton because she is female. However, he added,

> [T]he overwhelming majority of Americans are going to make these decisions based on who they think will be the best president. I have absolute confidence that if I'm doing my job, if I'm delivering my message, then there are very few voters out there that I can't win. If I'm not winning them over, then it's my fault.[36]

Deciding he needed to address the issue of race and the racial rhetoric, on March 18, 2008 at the National Constitution Center in Philadelphia, not far from where the Constitution of the United States was written, Barack made what many described as the most important speech on race in America since Dr. Martin Luther King's "I Have a Dream" speech. Speaking for nearly forty minutes, Barack confronted America's legacy of racial division and white resentment and urged America to overcome "a racial stalemate we've been stuck in for years." Barack said, "We have a choice in this country: we can accept a politics that breeds division, and conflict, and cynicism. Or, at this moment, we can come together and say: 'not this time.'" He added, "And today, whenever I find myself feeling doubtful or cynical about this possibility, what gives me the most hope is the next generation: the young people whose attitude and beliefs and openness to change have already made history in this election."[37]

After his speech on racial issues and rhetoric in Philadelphia, political strategists were quick to parse how the speech would affect his campaign and becoming the first black presidential nominee. Among African American scholars and leaders, the post-speech discussion was not of polls but of witnessing history. Reverend Alton Pollard, dean of Howard University's School of Divinity, said,

> This was his *kairos* moment [using the Greek word that characterizes moments that can alter destiny]. Race was never an issue that was going to disappear. It's too much a part of our national fabric to think that we can gloss over it and move on without having to contend mightily with each other.

Walter Earl Fluker, executive director of the Leadership Center at Morehouse College and a prominent voice in the black community, said the context of the speech was important for Americans to hear, and that it was different from the context of the 1960s when Martin Luther King delivered his famous "I Have a Dream" speech. "We have at least two, possibly three generations that have been born into this huge cultural void of memory [referring to Americans born between the 1960s and now]. So we take fragments of this past and base much of our understanding on these fragments." Fluker said that as the son of a black father and white mother, Barack had stepped into that cultural void and challenged the country to do better, not remain static, or fixed along racial lines.

> Senator Obama was clearly caught in that matrix, and he was the right person to be caught. Just as with Lincoln and Dr. King, you have in Obama a person who is able to stand in that gap at a moment when the nation is at one of its most difficult junctures. He has critiqued the grandiose way in which we've allowed race to play out, not just in politics, but in our day-to-day life. Like King in the past, and Franklin Delano Roosevelt during the Great Depression, he spoke directly to the complexity of the issue at hand, and translated it so it's a part of our nation's history.[38]

Barack's speech on race was delivered across the street from where the Constitution was written, and against a backdrop of American flags. Confronting the issue of race in America head-on, he also spoke sympathetically about the experiences of the white working class and the plight of workers who had lost their jobs and their retirement pensions.

Paul Finkelman, a professor at Albany Law School who has written about slavery, race, and the Constitution, said,

> As far as I know, he's the first politician since the Civil War to recognize how deeply embedded slavery and race have been in our Constitution. That's a profoundly important thing to say. But what's important about the way he said it is he doesn't use this as a springboard for anger or for frustration. He doesn't say, "O.K., slavery was bad, therefore people are owed something." This is not a reparations speech. This is a speech about saying it's time for the nation to do better, to form a more perfect union.

In the speech, Barack said, "Race is an issue that I believe this nation cannot afford to ignore right now." He said the controversies over the past couple of weeks

> reflect the complexities of race in this country that we've never really worked through—a part of our union that we have yet to perfect. And if we walk away now, if we simply retreat into our respective corners, we will never be able to come together and solve challenges like health care, or education, or the need to find good jobs for every American.[39]

In an interview with Dr. Cornel West, professor of religion and director of African American Studies at Princeton University, on the myth of "post-racial" politics and Obama's place in history, which appeared in the March 20, 2008 issue of *Rolling Stone* magazine, author Robert Boynton asked what West thought of those who say Barack is not "black enough," and Dr. West answered,

> When Obama first appeared on the scene, he was the darling of the white press, and that made black people suspicious. But when they had time to examine his record, his history, his relationship with Michelle Obama and his deep love for his precious children, the issue of "black enough" disappeared. That's why polls show him carrying eighty-five percent of the African-American vote.

Boynton asked if the nation should be worried about handing the reins of power to someone who is relatively inexperienced, or if that is just the kind of coded language that is always used to dismiss candidates of color. Dr. West said,

> I don't think it has much to do with Obama's race as with his youth … I don't think Obama is actually inexperienced when it comes to governing as president. He's going to choose a high quality team, and he has shown that he is capable of excellent political judgment.[40]

Secretary of State Condoleezza Rice has often been thought of as a potential candidate for president or vice president. Speaking about Barack's speech on race, she told the *Washington Post* on March 28, 2008,

> I think it was important that he [Obama] gave it for a whole host of reasons. There is a paradox for this country and a contradiction of this country and we still haven't resolved it. But what I would like understood as a black American is that black Americans loved and had faith in this country even when this country didn't love and have faith in them, and that's our legacy.[41]

In April 2008, Barack was interviewed on the cable news program *Fox News Sunday*. Barack said race would not be a factor in November's election that could make him the first black U.S. president. He added,

> Is race still a factor in our society? Yes. I don't think anybody would deny that. Is that going to be the determining factor in a general election? No, because I'm absolutely confident that the American people—what they're looking for is somebody who can solve their problems. I am confident that when you come to a general election, and we are having a debate about the future of this country … that those are voters who I will be able to appeal to. If I lose, it won't be because of race. It will be because … I made mistakes on the campaign trail, I wasn't communicating effectively my plans in terms of helping them in their everyday lives.[42]

On May 23, 2008, Barack was interviewed by CBS4, a television station in Florida. He was asked about the issue of prejudices among American voters. Barack said,

> I think an overwhelmingly majority of people are interested in a President who is interested in helping them live out of the American

dream. They're not concerned about whether it's a woman, or a black or a Hispanic; they just want to make sure that this person is working for them. This doesn't mean there aren't long standing prejudices on all sides, and I think my job is to let people know that I'm going to be their advocate, that I'm going to be fighting for you, regardless of where you come from … I want to make sure you can live out that American dream because that's what's been provided to me in this country.[43]

A June 7, 2008 editorial in the *Rocky Mountain News* said,

Obama is running on an agenda anchored not in activism on civil rights, but in issues of war, health care and the economy. He's a candidate who essentially tried to transcend racial concerns until the bigotry of his longtime former pastor forced him to face the question of race head on. But a major reason why Obama remains a decent bet to become the first African-American president is precisely because he *does* seem to personify the hope for a post-racial America and the yearnings of people of all backgrounds to rise above their differences.

Quoting *The Economist*, "For a country whose past is disfigured by slavery, segregation and unequal voting rights, this is a moment to celebrate. America's history of reinventing and perfecting itself has acquired another page."[44]

On Faith

I am hopeful that we can bridge the gaps that exist and overcome the prejudices each of us bring to this debate. And I have faith that millions of believing Americans want that to happen. No matter how religious they may or may not be, people are tired of seeing faith used as a tool of attack. They don't want faith used to belittle or to divide. They're tired of hearing folks deliver more screed than sermon. Because in the end, that's not how they think about faith in their own lives.

"Call to Renewal" keynote address, June 28, 2006.

Barack often speaks openly about his faith and he also embraces the separation of church and state. He was raised in a secular home and has described his mother as a deeply spiritual person. He writes in *The Audacity of Hope* that he was not raised in a religious household. The combination of traits, that of his grandmother's flinty rationalism and his grandfather's joviality and incapacity to judge others or himself too strictly, was passed along to his mother. She, Barack writes, provided him with no religious instruction, and that in her mind, it was a working knowledge of the world's great religions that was a necessary part of any well-rounded education. In his household were the Bible, the Koran, and the Bhagavad Gita, all of which sat on the shelf alongside books of Greek and Norse and African mythology.[45]

When he lived in Indonesia with his mother and stepfather, Barack attended a Catholic school for two years. For a short time, Barack attended a public school in Indonesia that was predominantly Muslim. When he moved to Chicago, Barack worked at a church-based community organization as an activist. It was the experiences in Chicago that forced him to confront the fact that he had no community or shared traditions to ground his most deeply held beliefs. In *The Audacity of Hope*, Barack wrote that the Christians that he worked with recognized themselves in him and they sensed that a part of him remained removed, detached, and an observer among them. He came to realize, he says, that "without a vessel for his beliefs, without an unequivocal commitment to a particular community of faith," he would be consigned to always remain apart, but also alone. Barack was drawn to the African American church traditions and realized that religious commitment did not require him to suspend critical thinking, disengage from the battle for economic and social justice, or otherwise retreat from the world that he knew and loved. He visited the Trinity United Church of Christ and was later baptized at the church. It came about as a choice, he says, not an epiphany. Barack writes that he felt "God's spirit beckoning" and "submitted myself to His will, and dedicated myself to discovering His truth."[46]

In November 2006, David Remnick interviewed Barack for *The New Yorker*. He was asked about his attitude about religion, about being raised in a secular home, and whether it was necessary for him to write about his religion in order to go to the next level in American politics. Barack said that what he was trying to describe is a

> faith that admits doubt, and uncertainty, and mystery ... I think that's how most people understand their faith. In fact, it's not faith if

you're absolutely certain. There's a leap that we all take, and, when you admit that doubt publicly, it's a form of testimony ... it allows both the secular and the religious to find some sort of common space where we say to each other ... I may not believe exactly what you do ... but I share an experience in wondering what does my life mean, or I understand the desire for a connection to something larger than myself. And that ... is in the best of the United States religious tradition.[47]

In April 2004, before he spoke at the Democratic National Convention and before he was a household name outside of Illinois, Barack was interviewed by Cathleen Falsani, a columnist for the *Chicago Sun Times*. Falsani asked him what he believed and Barack said he was a Christian and had a deep faith rooted in the Christian tradition. He believed, he said, "that there are many paths to the same place, a belief that there is a higher power, and that we are connected as a people. He said, "there are values that transcend race or culture ... an obligation for all of us individually as well as collectively to take responsibility to make those values lived." Barack described his father as an agnostic, his paternal grandfather as a Muslim, and his mother a Christian, "My mother ... was not someone who wore her religion on her sleeve ... she wasn't a 'church lady.'"

Barack told Falsani that along with his own deep personal faith, he was a follower of civic religion.

I am a big believer in the separation of church and state. I am a big believer in our constitutional structure ... I am a great admirer of our founding charter and its resolve to prevent theocracies from forming and its resolve to prevent disruptive strains of fundamentalism from taking root in this country.

He added that he thought there is an enormous danger on the part of public figures to rationalize or justify their actions by claiming God's mandate and that it is not healthy for public figures to wear their religion on their sleeve as a means of insulating themselves from criticism, or with dialogue with people who disagree with them. "The biggest challenge, I think, is always maintaining your moral compass." He added that he knows it is difficult for politicians to talk about faith and that part of the reason is that it is the nature of politics that you want everyone to admire you and see what is best about you. "Often times, that's by being as vague as possible, or appealing to the lower common denominators. The more specific and detailed you are on the issues as personal and fundamental as your faith, the more potentially dangerous it is."[48]

In January 2007, Cathleen Falsani once again interviewed Barack for the *Chicago Sun Times*. This time, she asked him if he was an evangelical. His answer was that he was not sure if labels are helpful because the definition of an evangelical is so loose and subject to so many different interpretations. He said,

> I came to Christianity through the black church tradition where the line between evangelical and non-evangelical is completely blurred. Nobody knows exactly what it means. Does it mean that you feel you've got a personal relationship with Christ the savior? Then that's directly part of the black church experience. Does it mean you're born-again in a classic sense, with all the accoutrements that go along with that, as it's understood by some other tradition? I'm not sure. My faith is complicated by the fact that I didn't grow up in a particular religious tradition. And so what that means is when you come at it as an adult, your brain mediates a lot, and you ask a lot of questions. There are aspects of Christian tradition that I'm comfortable with and aspects that I'm not. There are passages of the Bible that make perfect sense to me and others that I go, "Ya know, I'm not sure about that."[49]

In a televised forum on June 4, 2007, Senator John Edwards, Senator Hillary Clinton, and Senator Obama discussed religion and prayer in their lives. Barack tended to dwell somewhat on policy and global concerns, rather than on his personal faith or Scripture. But he also found ways to interlace religion and policy at the forum. Barack said it was important to remain "our brother's keeper, our sister's keeper to advance the causes of justice and freedom." He said he believed that evil existed in the world, noting, "I do think when planes crash into buildings and kill innocents, there's evil there." In other times of violence and war, however, he saw just causes, like the Civil War and the defeat of fascism and liberation of Europe. He also said that his "starting point as president is to restore the sense that we are in this together and that this commitment rose out of his faith." He promised to build alliances across partisan lines to improve early childhood education, children's nutrition, workers' pay, and efforts to put criminal offenders on a better path. "The notion that we take away education programs in prisons, to be tough on crime, makes absolutely no sense."[50]

On June 13, 2007, Barack wrote in a column entitled "Faith in Common Ground" that he had created an online community for people of faith to bring folks together around difficult issues and said,

> I think people are hungry for a different kind of politics—the kind of politics based on the ideals this country was founded upon. The idea that we are all connected as one people. That we all have a stake in one another. That there's room for pro-lifers and pro-choicers, Evangelicals and atheists, Democrats and Republicans and everyone in between, in this project of American renewal.[51]

Barack was raised in a nonreligious home and converted to Christianity as an adult. He said,

> I didn't have an epiphany. What I really did was to take a set of values and ideals that were first instilled in me from my mother, who was, as I have called her in my book, the last of the secular humanists—you know, belief in kindness and empathy and discipline, responsibility—those kinds of values. And I found in the Church a vessel or a repository for those values and a way to connect those values to a larger community and a belief in God and a belief in redemption and mercy and justice ... I guess the point is, it continues to be both a spiritual, but also intellectual, journey for me, this issue of faith.

In a June 2007 speech in Connecticut, Barack spoke about his religious conversion:

> One Sunday, I put on one of the few clean jackets I had, and went over to Trinity United Church of Christ ... and I heard a sermon called "The Audacity of Hope." ... During the course of that sermon, he [Reverend Jeremiah Wright] introduced me to someone named Jesus Christ. I learned that my sins could be redeemed ... those things I was too weak to accomplish myself, he would accomplish

with me if I placed my trust in him … I came to see faith as more than just a comfort to the weary or a hedge against death, but rather as an active, palpable agent in the world and in my own life … It came as a choice and not an epiphany. The questions I had didn't magically disappear. The skeptical bent of my mind didn't suddenly vanish … I heard God's spirit beckoning me.

In 2006, Barack said, "Faith doesn't mean that you don't have doubts."[52]

Two weeks before Barack announced his candidacy, he attended services at the Trinity United Church of Christ in Chicago. The church's motto is "unashamedly black and unapologetically Christian," and is the sort of church community that Barack wrote about wanting to connect with when he first came to Chicago as a community organizer. It is where he has said he found Christ, and it is where he and Michelle were married and where his two daughters were baptized. On that particular Sunday, among a sea of black worshippers, with a few white people in the balcony, many of whom were holding a copy of Barack's book *The Audacity of Hope*, Barack and his family were in the third row, sitting, standing, clapping, praying, and swaying along with the rest of the congregation. During the sermon, Barack listened intently and took notes. When the Reverend Jeremiah Wright, Jr. asked Barack to say a few words, Barack took the microphone and told the worshippers, "I love you all. It's good to be back home." The choir broke into a chorus of "Barack, Hallelujah! Barack, Hallelujah!"[53] In March 2008, after dated videos surfaced of the Reverend Wright's controversial and fiery comments about America, Barack was forced to confront the comments and distance himself from his long-time pastor who had retired from Chicago's Trinity United Church of Christ. On March 18, 2008, Barack made a speech on race to directly address the "firestorm" created by Wright and his views. The speech, made in Philadelphia at the National Constitution Center, was meant to make a sweeping assessment of race in America. Barack said he could not disown Wright, but made it clear that he condemned the comments. Wright continued to make comments and Barack continued to distance himself from them. In late May, Barack and Michelle resigned from the Church. Barack said,

Our relations with Trinity have been strained by the divisive statements of Reverend Wright, which sharply conflict with our own views. These controversies have served as an unfortunate distraction for other Trinity members who seek to worship in peace, and have placed you in an untenable position ... I make this decision with sadness. This is where I found Jesus Christ, where we were married, where our children were baptized. We are proud of the extraordinary works of that church ... I'm not denouncing the church, and I'm not interested in people who want me to denounce the church. It's not a church worthy of denouncing.[54]

Barack said on June 28, 2006, in his "Call to Renewal" keynote address,

This is why, if we truly hope to speak to people where they're at—to communicate our hopes and values in a way that's relevant to their own—we cannot abandon the field of religious discourse. Because when we ignore the debate about what it means to be a good Christian or Muslim or Jew; when we discuss religion only in the negative sense of where or how it should not be practiced, rather than in the positive sense of what it tells us about our obligations towards one another; when we shy away from religious venues and religious broadcasts because we assume that we will be unwelcome—others will fill the vacuum, those with the most insular views of faith, or those who cynically use religion to justify partisan ends.

NOTES

1. John K. Wilson, *Barack Obama, This Improbable Quest* (Boulder, CO: Paradigm Publishers, 2008), 53.
2. Michael A. Fletcher, "Obama's Appeal to Blacks Remains an Open Question," *Washington Post*, January 25, 2007, A01.
3. Marc Royce, "Oprah Talks to Barack Obama," *O, The Oprah Magazine*, November 2004, 248.
4. Lisa Rogak, ed. *Barack Obama, In His Own Words* (New York: Carroll & Graf Publishers, 2007), 106.
5. Steve Dougherty, *Hopes and Dreams, The Story of Barack Obama* (New York: Black Dog & Leventhal Publishers, Inc., 2007), 121.
6. Benjamin Wallace-Wells, "The Great Black Hope," *Washington Monthly*, November 2004, 30–36.
7. "*Newsweek* cover: Black and White," *Examiner.com*, July 8, 2007, http://www.examiner.com (accessed July 9, 2007).
8. David Ignatius, "Can Mr. Cool Get Hot?" *Washington Post*, October 11, 2007, A19.

9. Jonathan Kaufman, "Whites' Great Hope?" *Wall Street Journal*, November 10, 2007, A1.

10. Ronald Roach, "Obama Rising," *Black Issues in Higher Education*, 2004, 20–23.

11. Susan Page, "2008 Race Has the Face of a Changing America," *USA Today*, March 12, 2007.

12. Barack Obama, *The Audacity of Hope* (New York: Crown Publishers, 2006), 232–233.

13. Fox Butterfield, "First Black Elected to Head Harvard's Law Review," *New York Times*, February 6, 1990, A20.

14. Richard Wolffe and Darn Briscoe, "Across the Divide," *Newsweek*, July 16, 2007, 26.

15. Dawn Turner Trice, "Obama Unfazed by Foes' Doubts on Race Question," *Chicago Tribune*, March 15, 2004. Quoted in John K. Wilson, *Barack Obama, This Improbable Quest* (Boulder, CO: Paradigm Publishers, 2008), 56.

16. Noam Scheiber, "Race Against History," *New Republic*, May 31, 2004, 21–26.

17. Royce, "Oprah Talks to Barack Obama."

18. "Q & A with Senator Barack Obama," *Chicago Tribune*, June 30, 2005. General Reference Center Gold. Gale (accessed May 20, 2008).

19. Jonathan Alter, "The Challenges We Face," *Newsweek*, December 25, 2006, 36–40.

20. Fletcher, "Obama's Appeal to Blacks."

21. Steve Kroft, "Candidate Obama Feels 'Sense of Urgency,'" *60 Minutes*, February 11, 2007, http://www.il.proquest.com.ezproxy.denverlibrary.org (accessed May 9, 2008).

22. "Rice: Obama Candidacy Signals Progress," *Associated Press*, February 25, 2007, http://www.msnbc.msn.com (accessed February 26, 2007).

23. Susan Page, "2008 Race has the Face of a Changing America," *USA Today*, March 12, 2007, http://www.web.ebscohost.com (accessed July 26, 2007).

24. Patrick Healy, "Courting Black Votes, Obama Emphasizes Principles, *New York Times*, April 22, 2007, 1.25.

25. Shamus Toomey, "A Lot to Do with Race," *Chicago Sun Times*, May 5, 2007, http://www.suntimes.com (accessed May 18, 2007).

26. Ron Walters, "Barack Obama and the Politics of Blackness," *Journal of Black Studies*, July 18, 2007, 17.

27. Ibid.

28. Gary Younge, "The Obama Effect," *The Nation*, December 31, 2007.

29. "*Newsweek* cover: Black and White."

30. Karen Tumulty, "Our of Reach?" *Time*, October 8, 2007, 51.

31. Gwen Ifill, "The Candidate," *Essence*, October 2007, 224.

32. Kaufman, "Whites' Great Hope?"

33. Barack Obama, "Transcript of February 12 Speech," *New York Times*, February 12, 2008, http://www.nytimes.com (accessed February 14, 2008).

34. Kenneth T. Walsh, "One-on-One with Barack Obama," *U.S. News & World Report*, February 25, 2008, 44.

35. Matthew Bigg, "Black Americans See Obama Rise in Context of History," *Reuters*, February 28, 2008, http://news.yahoo.com (accessed February 28, 2008).

36. "Obama: Voters to Judge Issues, Not Race," *Associated Press*, March 13, 2008, http://ap.google.com (accessed March 13, 2008).

37. Tom Baldwin, "Barack Obama Attacks US State of 'Racial Stalemate,'" *Times Online*, March 19, 2008, http://www.timesonline.co.uk/tol/news/world/us_and_americas/us_electives/article3578425.ece (accessed March 19, 2008).

38. Liz Halloran, "Obama's Race Speech Heralded as Historic," *U.S. News & World Report*, March 18, 2008, http://www.usnews.com (accessed March 18, 2008).

39. Janny Scott, "Obama Chooses Reconciliation Over Rancor," *New York Times*, March 19, 2008, A.14.

40. Robert S. Boynton, "Obama and the Blues," *Rolling Stone*, March 20, 2008, 42.

41. Sue Pleming, "Rice Hails Obama Race Speech as 'Important' for U.S." *Reuters*, March 28, 2008, http://news.yahoo.com (accessed March 28, 2008).

42. "Obama Says Race Not an Issue in U.S. Election," *Reuters*, April 27, 2008, http://www.nytimes.com (accessed April 27, 2008).

43. "CBS4's One-On-One Interview with Barack Obama," *CBS4.com*, May 23, 2008, http://www.cbs4.com (accessed May 23, 2008).

44. Editorial, "History in the Making," *Rocky Mountain News*, June 7, 2008, 29.

45. Obama, *The Audacity of Hope*, 202–204.

46. Ibid., 206, 208.

47. David Remnick, "Testing the Waters," *New Yorker*, November 6, 2006, http://www.newyorker.com (accessed May 30, 2008).

48. Cathleen Falsani, "Obama: I Have a Deep Faith," *Chicago Sun-Times*, April 5, 2004, http://www.suntimes.com (accessed June 11, 2008).

49. Cathleen Falsani, "Evangelical? Obama's Faith Too Complex for Simple Label," *Chicago Sun-Times*, January 19, 2007, http://www.suntimes.com (accessed June 11, 2008).

50. Patrick Healy and Michael Luo, "Edwards, Clinton and Obama Describe Journeys of Faith," *New York Times*, June 5, 2007, A20.

51. Barack Obama, "Faith on Common Ground," *Washington Post*, June 13, 2007, http://www.washingtonpost.com (accessed June 13, 2007).

52. Andrew Sullivan, "Goodbye to All That," *The Atlantic*, December 2007, 49.

53. Ryan Lizza, "The Agitator," *New Republic*, March 19, 2007, http://www.tnr.com (accessed June 5, 2008).

54. Michael Powell, "Following Months of Criticism, Obama Quits His Church," *New York TimesOnline*, June 1, 2008, http://www.nytimes.com (accessed June 1, 2008).

Conclusion

"America, this is our moment. This is our time, our time to turn the page on the policies of the past ... our time to bring new energy and new ideas to the challenges we face, our time to offer a new direction for this country that we love. The journey will be difficult. The road will be long. I face this challenge—I face this challenge with profound humility and knowledge of my own limitations, but I also face it with limitless faith in the capacity of the American people. Because if we are willing to work for it, and fight for it, and believe in it, then I am absolutely certain that, generations from now, we will be able to look back and tell our children that this was the moment when we began to provide care for the sick and good jobs to the jobless ... this was the moment when the rise of the oceans began to slow and our planet began to heal ... this was the moment when we ended a war, and secured our nation, and restored our image as the last, best hope on Earth. This was the moment, this was the time when we came together to remake this great nation so that it may always reflect our very best selves and our highest ideals."[1]

The Presumptive Democratic Nominee for the Presidency

On Tuesday, June 3, 2008, Barack became the presumptive nominee for the Democratic Party. The final two primaries, in Montana, where Barack prevailed, and in South Dakota, where Hillary Clinton won the most votes, pushed Barack over the edge in pledged delegates. With his win in Montana and with his share of the South Dakota delegates, most of the uncommitted superdelegates then voiced their support. According to the Associated Press, Barack sealed his nomination on the basis of primary elections, state Democratic caucuses, and support from party superdelegates. His nomination concluded a seventeen-month marathon for the Democratic nomination. All told, there were fifty-four contests, hundreds of millions of dollars spent, and at the end, the race remained too close to call; it was the longest nomination race in history.

From the beginning, even before he announced his candidacy in February 2007, many called Barack's campaign improbable. Few said it could be done, and fewer still felt he could become the nominee against the formidable Hillary Clinton, who early on was called the odds-on favorite to be the nominee. On Tuesday, June 3, Barack made a historic claim to the Democratic presidential nomination. He was the first African American in this country's history to do so. And although she did not concede, and while she signaled that she was open to being Barack's running mate, Hillary Clinton, who would have been the first female presidential nominee in history, saluted Barack in her speech that evening. She had all along stated she was the most electable candidate, given her support among women, white men, older voters, and blue-collar workers. Many superdelegates did not agree and cast their endorsement and their vote for Barack. Among those superdelegates that cast their votes early on the day of the final primary was Representative Jim Clyburn of South Carolina. Clyburn, a civil-rights-era leader and the House of Representatives senior African American, said Barack "has created levels of energy and excitement that I have not witnessed since the 1960s," especially among younger voters.

I believe he is the most electable candidate that Democrats can offer. He will be able to dramatically change the electoral map for Democrats which will in turn expand our majorities here in Congress, and help elect more Democrats at the state and local levels.

Other politicians stated that Barack should be the party's nominee because he would draw young voters, African Americans, and other new Democrats and independents to the polls in the November election.

To an estimated crowd of 32,000 people in the Xcel Energy Center in St. Paul, Minnesota, the site of the Republican National Convention in September, Barack said, "Tonight, I can stand before you and say that I will be the Democratic nominee for president of the United States of America." The venue symbolized the beginning of the general election campaign against John McCain, the presumptive Republican nominee, who clinched the nomination months before. McCain also spoke that evening in New Orleans, and said, "Both Senator Obama and I promise we will end Washington's stagnant, unproductive partisanship. But one of us has a record of working to do that, and one of us doesn't." Barack, for his part, complimented Senator McCain on his military service and his "many accomplishments—even if he chooses to deny mine. My differences with him are not personal; they are with the policies he has proposed in this campaign," policies that Barack said would amount to four more years of President Bush's policies.[2]

On June 4, 2008, the day after he was named the presumptive nominee for the Democratic Party, Barack and Hillary Clinton spoke at the Pro-Israel conference for the American Israel Public Affairs Committee, known as AIPAC. According to the *Huffington Post*, on June 4, some observers noted that Barack faced the prospect of a cool reception during his speech at the conference. After receiving a massive ovation upon entering the crowd's view at the convention center in Washington, D.C., Barack, the *Post* noted, apparently felt comfortable enough to meet any residual doubts about his record on Israel's security with a touch of humor and then a great many specifics. After Barack spoke, it was Senator Clinton's turn. She had yet to concede the race to Barack, had yet to endorse him, and had not suspended or quit her campaign. She said in her speech at the conference,

Let me be clear. I know that Senator Obama will be a good friend to Israel. I know Senator Obama shares my view that the next president must be ready to say to the world. Our position is unchanging, our resolve unyielding, our stance non-negotiable. The United States stands with Israel, now and forever.[3]

On Saturday, June 8, 2008, after much speculation about what she would do, Hillary Clinton made a speech at the historic National Building Museum in Washington, D.C. In her speech, she brought her campaign for the White House to an end with a rousing farewell. Standing alone on the stage, she spoke about the importance of electing Barack as president, and about the extent to which her campaign was a milestone for women. She made an unequivocal call for her voters to get behind Barack, the man who had defeated her for the nomination. She asked her supporters not to take the wrong lesson from her loss. She said,

> You can be proud that, from now on, it will be unremarkable for a woman to win primary state victories, unremarkable to have a woman in a close race to be our nominee, unremarkable to think that a woman can be the president of the United States. To those who are disappointed that we couldn't go all the way, especially the young people who put so much into this campaign, it would break my heart if, in falling short of my goal, I in any way discouraged any of you from pursuing yours.

It took Senator Clinton seven minutes into the speech to first mention Barack, but when she did, she swept away doubt that she was ready to concede or that she was hesitant about endorsing him or his qualifications to be president. She said,

> The way to continue our fight now, to accomplish the goals for which we stand, is to take our energy, our passion, our strength and do all we can to help elect Barack Obama the next president of the United States ... I congratulate him on the victory he has won and the extraordinary race he has run. I endorse him and throw my full support behind him.

The crowd roared with their approval when Hillary said Barack's name, but there were some boos and jeers as well. She told the crowd and supporters across the nation to join her in working hard for Barack and that she had campaigned with him for sixteen months, had stood on the same stage with him, and had gone toe-to-toe with him in twenty-two debates; she said she had had a front row seat to his candidacy and had seen his determination, his grace, and his grit. She reminded her supporters that it would take all their strength and energy to help elect Barack as president and added, "So today I am standing with Senator Obama to say, 'Yes, we can!'" Barack, in Chicago, responded quickly to the speech and paid tribute to the message and thanked her for her support. "I honor her today for the valiant and historic campaign she has run. She shattered barriers on behalf of my daughters and women everywhere, who now know that there are no limits to their dreams." The event was in many ways a traditional end to a campaign that never had a traditional beginning. Unlike Barack, who announced his candidacy in February 2007 in front of a huge crowd in Springfield, Illinois in a speech that was full of symbolism in front the old Illinois State Capitol building where Abraham Lincoln had served and lived, Hillary announced her campaign in January 2007 by posting an announcement on the Internet.[4]

Now that he was the presumptive nominee for the Democratic Party, Barack and rival John McCain kicked off their battle for the presidency. Amid the Iraq war, the war in Afghanistan, a sinking economy that was affecting most Americans with job losses, high gas prices, unaffordable health care; skyrocketing food prices, and all of the other problems facing the country, there were vast differences between the two candidates; however, they both were promising change. Both began the day hoping to frame the campaign ahead. Barack tied McCain's campaign to President Bush, whose approval ratings ranged from 25 percent to 30 percent, based on various polls. McCain said, "No matter who wins this election, the direction of this country is going to change dramatically." He vowed a new direction on a list of issues and said, "I've worked with the president to keep our nation safe. But he and I have not seen eye to eye on many issues." Barack answered, "There are many words to describe John McCain's attempt to pass off his embrace of George Bush's policies as bipartisan and new. But change is not one of them." Barack and John McCain are as different as their individual backgrounds. Barack, at forty-six years old, is a one-term senator who went from Harvard Law School to community organizing on the streets of Chicago. Senator McCain, a Vietnam war hero, is the son and grandson of admirals and has served a quarter of a century in Congress. At seventy-two years of age, and with thinning white hair, if he is elected president, he will be the oldest president sworn in for a first term. With these differences, both promise change in how Washington works. Barack promises to reach across the aisle, lower the rhetoric, and seek common ground where possible. Senator McCain vows to do the same. Barack said, "I'll reach my hand out to anyone, Republican or Democrat, who will help me change what needs to be changed. We may call ourselves Democrats and Republicans, but we are Americans first. We are always Americans first."[5]

NOTES

1. Barack Obama, "Remarks in St. Paul, Minnesota," Transcript. *CQ Today Online News*, June 3, 2008, http://www.cqpolitics.com (accessed June 4, 2008).
2. Jackie Calmes, "Obama Clinches Nomination, Capping Historic, Bitter Contest," *New York Times*, June 4, 2008, A1, A4.
3. "Daily Brief," *Huffington Post*, June 4, 2008, http://www.huffingtonpost.com (accessed June 4, 2008).
4. Adam Nagourney and Mark Leibovich, "Clinton Ends Bid with Clear Call to Elect Obama," *New York Times*, June 8, 2008, A. 1.
5. Laura Meckler, "McCain, Obama Kick Off Groundbreaking Battle," *Wall Street Journal*, June 4, 2008, A4.

Bibliography

"A Fighter in Search of an Opponent." *The Economist*, February 9, 2008, 30.

Allen, Mike, and Ben Smith. "Liberal Views Could Haunt Obama." *USA Today*, December 12, 2007, http://www.usatoday.com (accessed December 12, 2007).

Alter, Jonathan. "The Challenges We Face." *Newsweek*, December 25, 2006, 36–40.

———. "Is America Ready?" *Newsweek*, December 25, 2006, 28–35.

———. "Obama Plays Offense." *Newsweek*, February 4, 2008, 32.

Alter, Jonathan, and Daren Brisco. "The Audacity of Hope." *Newsweek*, December 27, 2004, 74–87.

Aminder, Marc. "Teacher and Apprentice." *The Atlantic*, December 2007, 59–60, 64.

Asante, Molefi Kete. "Barack Obama and the Dilemma of Power." *Journal of Black Studies*, 48, no. 1 (2007), 105–115.

Astill, James. "The Campaign's Brightest Star." *The Economist*, June 16, 2007, 33.

Bacon, Perry, Jr. "The Exquisite Dilemma of Being Obama." *Time*, February 20, 2006, 24.

Baldwin, Tom. "Barack Obama Attacks U.S. State of 'Racial Stalemate.'" *Times Online*, March 19, 2008, http://www.timesonline.co.uk (accessed March 19, 2008).

Baldwin, Tom, and Tim Reid. "I'm Winning this Race, Barack Obama Says, So Why Should I Be No. 2?" *Times Online*, March 11, 2008, http://www.timesonline.co.uk (accessed March 11, 2008).

Balz, Dan. "With Campaign Underway, Obama Now Must Show More Than Potential." *Washington Post*, February 13, 2007, A09.

———. "Obama Says He Can United U.S. 'More Effectively' Than Clinton." *Washington Post*, August 15, 2007, A01.

Barabak, Mark Z. "Ex-Labor Secretary Reich Backs Obama." *Los Angeles Times*, April 19, 2008, http://www.latimes.com (accessed April 19, 2008).

"Barack Obama Foreign Policy." *On The Issues.* http://www.ontheissues.org (accessed June 2, 2008).

"Barack Obama Jumps into 2008 Race." *CBS News Online*, January 16, 2007, http://www.cbsnews.com (accessed January 16, 2007).

Bartiromo, Maria. "Facetime with Barack Obama." *Business Week Online*, April 3, 2008, http://www.businessweek.com (accessed April 3, 2008).

Baxter, Tom, and Saeed Ahemed. "20,000 Turn Out for Obama." *Atlanta Journal Constitution*, April 14, 2007, http://www.ajc.com (accessed April 15, 2007).

Bigg, Matthew. "Black Americans See Obama Rise in Context of History." *Reuters*, February 28, 2008, http://news.yahoo.com (accessed February 28, 2008).

Borger, Gloria. "Does Barack Really Rock?" *U.S. News & World Report*, November 6, 2006, 43.

Boynton, Robert S. "Obama and the Blues." *Rolling Stone*, March 20, 2008, 42.

Briscoe, Daren. "Black and White." *Newsweek*, July 8, 2007.

Broder, John M. "Shushing the Baby Boomers." *New York Times*, January 21, 2007, 1, 14.

Brooks, David. "The Obama-Clinton Issue." *New York Times*, December 18, 2007, A.35.

———. "The Two Earthquakes." *New York Times*, January 4, 2008, A.19.

Brown, Carrie Budoff. "Obama Asks Jewish Voters for Chance." *Politico.com*, May 23, 2008, http://www.politico.com (accessed May 26, 2008).

Brozyna, Christine. "Get to Know Barack Obama." *ABC News Online*, November 1, 2007, http://www.abcnews.com (accessed November 21, 2007).

Bryant, Nick. "A Black Man in the White House?" *BBC News*, July 3, 2007, http://news.bbc.co.uk (accessed July 3, 2007).

Burnside, Randolph, and Kami Whitehurst. "From the Statehouse to the White House? Barack Obama's Bid to Become the Next President." *Journal of Black Studies*, July 31, 2007, 75.

Butterfield, Fox. "First Black Elected to Head Harvard's Law Review." *New York Times*, February 6, 1990, A.20.

Calmes, Jackie. "Democrats' Litmus: Electability: Key Issue for 2008 Race Poses Hurdles for Clinton, Obama." *Wall Street Journal*, January 11, 2007, A6.

———. "Obama Clinches Nomination, Capping Historic, Bitter Contest." *New York Times*, June 4, 2008, A.1, A.4.

"The Campaign's Brightest Star." *The Economist*, June 16, 2007, 33–34.

Cannellos, Peter S. "On Affirmative Action, Obama Intriguing but Vague." *Boston Globe*, April 29, 2008, http://www.boston.com (accessed April 29, 2008).

Carlson, Margaret. "For Obama, It's Public Character That Counts." *Bloomberg News*, January 4, 2007, http://www.bloomberg.com (accessed January 4, 2007).

Chaudhry, Lakshmi. "Will the Real Generation Obama Please Stand Up?" *The Nation*, November 15, 2007, http://news.yahoo.com (accessed November 16, 2007). Article appeared in the December 3, 2007 edition of *The Nation*.

Clayton, Jonathan, and Nyangoma Kogela. "Favourite Son Is Already a Winner in Kenya." *Times of London*, February 10, 2007, http://elibrary.bigchalk.com (accessed February 12, 2007).

Clayworth, Jason. "Obama Victory Speech: 'Time for Change Has Come.'" *Des Moines Register*, January 4, 2008, http://www.desmoinesregister.com (accessed January 4, 2008).

Cohen, Roger. "Obama's Youth-Drive Movement." *New York Times*, January 28, 2008, http://www.nytimes.com (accessed January 28, 2008).

Crummy, Karen. "Obama: 'The Country Calls Us.'" *Denver Post*, March 19, 2007, 1B, 5B.

"Daily Brief." *Huffington Post*, June 4, 2008, http://www.huffingtonpost.com (accessed June 4, 2008).

Davey, Monica. "As Quickly as Overnight, a Democratic Star Is Born." *New York Times*, March 18, 2004, A.20.

"Day 2 of 'Oprahpalooza' begins in SC." *Associated Press*, December 9, 2007, http://www.msnbc.msn.com (accessed December 10, 2007).

Devaney, Sherri, and Mark Devaney. *Barack Obama*. Farmington Hills, MI: Thompson Gale, 2007.

DeYoung, Karen. "Obama and Romney Lay Out Positions on Iraq and Beyond." *Washington Post*, May 31, 2007, A10.

De Zutter, Hank. "What Makes Obama Run?" *Chicago Reader*, December 8, 1995, http://www.chicagoreader.com (accessed June 3, 2008).

Dickinson, Tim. "The Machinery of Hope." *Rolling Stone*, March 20, 2008, 38.

Dorsey, Margaret E., and Miguel Diaz-Barriga. "Senator Barack Obama and Immigration Reform." *Journal of Black Studies*, July 18, 2007, http://jbs.sagepub.com (accessed July 18, 2007).

Dougherty, Steve. *Hopes and Dreams, The Story of Barack Obama*. New York: Black Dog & Leventhal Publishers, Inc., 2007.

Drew, Christopher, and Mike McIntire. "Obama Built Donor Network from Roots Up." *New York Times*, April 3, 2007.

Duffy, Michael. "Obama Moves On, Without a Bounce." *Time*, January 9, 2008.

Editorial, "History in the Making." *Rocky Mountain News*, June 7, 2008, 29.

Enda, Jodi. "Great Expectations." *American Prospect*, February 5, 2006, http://www.prospect.org (accessed January 29, 2007).

Falsani, Cathleen. "Obama: I Have a Deep Faith." *Chicago Sun Times*, April 5, 2004, http://www.suntimes.com (accessed June 11, 2008).

———. "Evangelical? Obama's Faith Too Complex for Simple Label." *Chicago Sun Times*, January 19, 2007, http://www.suntimes.com (accessed June 11, 2008).

Ferguson, Andrew. "The Literary Obama." *Weekly Standard*, February 12, 2007.

Fletcher, Michael. "Obama's Appeal to Blacks Remains an Open Question." *Washington Post*, January 26, 2007, A01.

"For the Democrats: Obama." *Chicago Tribune*, January 27, 2008, http://www.chicagotribune.com (accessed January 28, 2008).

Foulkes, Toni, "Case Study: Chicago-The Barack Obama Campaign." *Social Policy*, Winter 34, Spring 34, no. 2, 3 (2003, 2004),: 49–51.

Fournier, Ron. "The Unknown: Is Obama Ready?" *Associated Press*, June 17, 2007, http://news.yahoo.com (accessed June 18, 2007).

———. "Obama Presidency a 'Stretch' for Voters." *Associated Press*, August 21, 2007, http://abcnews.go.com (accessed August 21, 2007).

Gensheimer, Lydia. "Big Crowd, Big Win for Obama in Heart of Des Moines." *CQ Today*, January 4, 2008, http://www.cqpolitics.com (accessed January 4, 2008).

Gerson, Michael. "A Phenom with Flaws." *Washington Post*, May 23, 2008, http://www.washingtonpost.com (accessed May 26, 2008).

"Getting Fratricidal." *The Economist*, March 15, 2008, 38.

Giroux, Greg. "Obama and Huckabee Score Upsets in Iowa." *CQ Today*, January 4, 2008.

Goldberg, Jeffrey. "The Starting Gate." *New Yorker*, January 15, 2007, http://www.newyorker.com (accessed May 23, 2008).

Green, David. "Candidacy Status: Sen. Barack Obama (IL)." *National Public Radio*, July 9, 2007, http://www.npr.org (accessed July 9, 2007).

Greenberg, David. "How Obama is Like JFK." *Washington Post*, April 20, 2007.

Grim, Ryan. "Obama's World." *The Politico*, March 6, 2007, http://www.cbsnews.com. (accessed March 6, 2007).

Griscom, Amanda. "Muckraker." *Salon*, August 6, 2004, http://www.salon.com (accessed May 29, 2008).

Halloran, Liz. "Obama's Race Speech Heralded as Historic." *U.S. News & World Report*, March 18, 2008, http://www.usnews.com (accessed March 18, 2008).

Harwood, John. "In Superdelegate Count, Tough Math for Clinton." *New York Times*, April 7, 2008, A18.

Healy, Patrick. "Courting Black Votes, Obama Emphasizes Principles." *New York Times*, April 22, 2007, 1.25.

———. "Obama Disputes Claim of Sharing Clinton's Stance on War." *New York Times*, May 18, 2007, A22.

Healy, Patrick, and Michael Luo. "Edwards, Clinton and Obama Describe Journeys of Faith." *New York Times*, June 5, 2007, A20.

Hession, Gregory A. "Barack Obama." *The New American*, May 26, 2008, 22.

Hunter, Jennifer. "Obama Brushes Off Race Question." *Chicago Sun Times*, December 2, 2007, http://www.suntimes.com (accessed December 7, 2007).

Ifill, Gwen. "On the Road with Michelle." *Essence*, September 7, 2007, 203–206.

———. "The Candidate." *Essence*, October 2007, 224.

Ignatius, David. "Can Mr. Cool Get Hot?" *Washington Post*, October 11, 2007, A19.

Kantor, Jodi. "In Law School, Obama Found Political Voice." *New York Times*, January 28, 2007. 1, 21.

———. "A Candidate, His Minister and the Search for Faith." *New York Times*, April 30, 2007, A.1.

Kantor, Jodi, and Jeff Zeleny. "Michele Obama Adds New Role to Balancing Act." *New York Times*, May 18, 2007, A1.

Kaufman, Jonathan. "Whites' Great Hope?" *Wall Street Journal*, November 10, 2007, A1.

Keating, Stephen. "Obama Moms Cradle Campaign." *Denver Post*, June 10, 2007, C03.

Keen, Judy. "Candid and Unscripted, Campaigning Her Way." *USA Today*, May 11, 2007, 01a.

Kennedy, Caroline. "A President Like My Father." *New York Times*, January 27, 2008. WK.18.

Klein, Joe. "The Fresh Face." *Time*, October 23, 2006, 44.

———. "How to Build a Bonfire." *Time*, February 26, 2007, 18.

———. "Barack Obama." *Time*, May 14, 2007, 57–58.

———. "Obama's History Victory." *Time*, January 4, 2008.

———. "Obama's Challenge—and Ours." *Time*, March 31, 2008, 31.

———. "Petraeus Meets His Match." *Time*, April 21, 2008, 29.

Klein, Richard, and Nancy Flores. "The Note: Double-Oh Show." *ABC News Online*, December 7, 2007, http://abcnews.com (accessed December 7, 2007).

Kornblut, Anne E., and Shailagh Murray. "I'm Tired of Politics as Usual." *Washington Post*, December 9, 2007, A01.

Krawczeniuk, Borys. "Interview with Barack Obama." *Scranton Times-Tribune*, April 21, 2008, http://www.timesshamrock.com (accessed April 21, 2008).

Kristof, Nicholas D. "Obama: Man of the World." *New York Times*, March 6, 2007, A.21.

Kuhnhenn, Jim, and Charles Babington. "Bitter Words Spur Debate." *Denver Post*, April 13, 2008, 21A.

La Ganga, Maria L. "Obama Has New Rallying Cry: Yes, We Can!" *Los Angeles Times*, January 9, 2008.

Liebowitz, Sarah. "Democrats Pick Clinton." *Concord Monitor*, January 9, 2008, http://www.concordmonitor.com (accessed January 9, 2008).

Little, Amanda Griscom. "Barack Obama." *Rolling Stone*, December 30, 2004, 88.

———. "Obama on Energy for' 08." *Salon*, August 27, 2007, http://www.salon.com (accessed May 29, 2008).

Littwin, Mike. "Still Waiting for Obama to Deliver Something New." *Rocky Mountain News*, November 17, 2007, 30.

Lizza, Ryan. "The Natural." *Atlantic Monthly*, September 2004, 30–33.

———. "The Agitator." *New Republic*, March 19, 2007, http://www.tnr.com (accessed June 5, 2008).

———. "Above the Fray." *GQ*, September 2007, 334, 335–337, 408–409.

MacFarquhar, Larissa. "The Conciliator." *The New Yorker*, May 7, 2007, http://www.newyorker.com (accessed December 18, 2007).

———. "Ask the Author: Larissa MacFarquhar: "The Conciliator." *The New Yorker*, May 14, 2007.

Marcus, Ruth. "The Clintonian Candidate." *Washington Post*, January 31, 2007, A15.

———. "From Barack Obama, Two Dangerous Words." *Washington Post*, July 11, 2007, A15.

McClelland, Edward. "How Obama Learned to be a Natural." *Salon*, February 12, 2007, http://www.salon.com (accessed May 12, 2008).

McGirt, Ellen. "The Brand Called Obama." *Fast Company*, April 2008, 87–88, 92.

Meckler, Laura. "McCain, Obama Kick Off Groundbreaking Battle." *Wall Street Journal*, June 4, 2008, A4.

Mendell, David. *Obama: From Promise to Power*. New York: Amistad, 2007.

Merida, Kevin. "The Ghost of a Father." *Washington Post*, December 14, 2007, A12.

Merrion, Paul. "Obama's Appeal Drives Cash Flow." *Paul Crain's Chicago Business*, September 15, 2003.

Moberg, David. "Obama's Community Roots." *The Nation*, April 3, 2007, 16, 18.

Mosk, Matthew, and John Solomon. "Obama Taps Two Worlds to Fill 2008 War Chest." *Washington Post*, April 15, 2007, A01.

Mundy, Liza. "A Series of Fortunate Events." *Washington Post*, August 12, 2007, W10.

Nagourney, Adam. "Obama Made Inroads, but Fervor Fell Short." *New York Times*, February 7, 2008, http://msnbc.msn.com (accessed February 7, 2008).

———. "Surging, Obama Makes His Case." *New York Times*, February 13, 2008, A.21.

———. "2 Years After Big Speech, a Lower Key for Obama." *New York Times*, April 8, 2007, 15.

Nagourney, Adam, and Mark Leibovich. "Clinton Ends Bid with Clear Call to Elect Obama." *New York Times*, June 8, 2008, A.1.

Nagourney, Adam, and Jeff Zeleny. "Obama Formally Enters Presidential Race with Calls for Generational Change." *New York Times*, February 11, 2007, 22.

"*Newsweek* Cover: Black and White." *Examiner.com*, July 8, 2007, http://www.examiner.com (accessed July 9, 2007).

Noonan, Peggy. "The Man from Nowhere." *Wall Street Journal*, December 16, 2006, 14.

Norment, Lynn. "The Hottest Couple in America." *Ebony*, February 1, 2007, 52.

Norris, Michele. "Michelle Obama Sees Election as Test for America." *National Public Radio*, July 9, 2007, http://www.npr.org (accessed July 9, 2007).

Obama, Barack. *Dreams from My Father*. New York: Three Rivers Press, 2004.

———. *The Audacity of Hope*. New York: Crown Publishers, 2006.

———. "Remarks: Governor's Ethanol Coalition, Energy Security is National Security." February 28, 2006, http://obama.senate.gov (accessed May 29, 2008).

———. "Remarks: Energy Independence and the Safety of Our Planet." April 3, 2006, http://obama.senate.gov (accessed May 29, 2008).

———. "Floor Statement: Employment Verification Amendment for the Immigration Bill." May 23, 2006, http://obama.senate.gov (accessed May 29, 2008).

———. "Floor Statement: Amendment Requiring a Photo ID to Vote." May 24, 2006, http://obama.senate.gov (accessed May 29, 2008).

———. "Floor Statement: Federal Marriage Amendment." June 5, 2006, http://obama.senate.gov (accessed May 29, 2008).

———. "Presidential Exploratory Committee." http://www.barackobama.com, (accessed January 16, 2007).

———. Steve Kroft, "Candidate Obama Feels 'Sense of Urgency,'" *60 Minutes*, February 11, 2007, http://www.il.proquest.com.ezproxy.denverlibrary.org (accessed May 9, 2008).

———. "Faith on Common Ground." *Washington Post*, June 13, 2007, http://www.washingtonpost.com (accessed June 13, 2007).

———. "Renewing American Leadership." *Foreign Affairs*, July/August 2007, http://www.foreignaffairs.org (accessed June 5, 2007).

———. "A New Beginning." October 2, 2007, http://www.barackobama.com (accessed October 3, 2007).

———. "Obama '08." http://my.barackobama.com (accessed October 3, 2007).

———. "Major Speech on Iraq." http://www.barackobama.com (accessed October 3, 2007).

———. "On the Issues." http://www.barackobama.com (accessed December 20, 2007).

———. "Caucus Speech." *New York Times*, January 3, 2008, http://www.nytimes.com (accessed January 7, 2008).

———. "Remarks: New Hampshire Primary." January 8, 2008, http://thepage.time.com (accessed January 9, 2008).

———. "Concession Speech." January 9, 2008, http//thepage.time.com (accessed January 9, 2008).

———. "February 12 Speech." *New York Times*, February 12, 2008, http://www.nytimes.com (accessed February 14, 2008).

———. "A More Perfect Union." March 18, 2008, http://www.barackobama.com (accessed March 19, 2008).

———. "Remarks: Indiana's Jefferson Jackson Dinner, May 4, 2008." http://www.presidency.ucsb.edu (accessed July 8, 2008).

———. "Remarks: Raleigh, North Carolina, May 6, 2008." http://www.presidency.ucsb.edu (accessed July 8, 2008).

———. "Wesleyan Commencement Address, May 25, 2008." *WFSB.com*, http://www.wfsb.com (accessed May 25, 2008).

———. "Issues-Healthcare." http://www.barackobama.com (accessed May 29, 2008).

———. "Remarks: St. Paul, Minnesota." *CQ Today Online*, June 3, 2008, http://www.cqpolitics.com (accessed June 4, 2008).

"Obama: Voters to Judge Issues, Not Race." *Associated Press*, March 13, 2008, http://ap.google.com (accessed March 13, 2008).

"Obama Well-Traveled in Brief Senate Career." *CNN.com*, February 2, 2007, http://www.cnn.com/2007/politics/02/15 (accessed February 2, 2007).

"Obama Says He Is Emissary for Change." *Associated Press*, July 5, 2007, http://www.msnbc.msn.com (accessed July 5, 2007).

"Obama Says Race Not an Issue in U.S. Election." *Reuters*, April 27, 2008, http://www.nytimes.com (accessed April 27, 2008).

"Obama Would Tax Wealthy to Pay for Universal Health Care." *CNN*, May 30, 2007, http://cnn.worldnews.com (accessed May 30, 2007).

"Obamamania." *The Economist*, October 28, 2006, 42.

"Obamamania." *The Economist*, January 12, 2008, 26.

"Obama's Moment." *The Economist*, December 1, 2007, 46.

"Obama's Second Coming." *The Economist*, November 6, 2004, 33.

"On the Campaign Trail, Primary Colour." *The Economist*, March 15, 2008, 38.

Page, Susan. "2008 Race Has the Face of a Changing America." *USA Today*, March 12, 2007, 01a.

Pallasch, Abdon M. "Democratic Primary: Obama Urges Parents to Limit Children's Video Game Time." *Chicago Sun Times*, May 1, 2008, http://www.suntimes.com (accessed May 1, 2008).

Pearson, Rick. "Obama on Obama." *Chicago Tribune*, December 15, 2006, http://www.chicagotribune.com (accessed May 19, 2008).

Pelofsky, Jeremy. "Sen. Obama Nears Clinton in Campaign Money Race." *Reuters*, April 4, 2007, http://news.yahoo.com (accessed April 4, 2007).

Pickler, Nedra. "Winfrey, Clinton Kin Draw Crowds of Iowa Women." *Denver Post*, December 9, 2007, 8a.

Pierce, Charles P. "The Cynic and Senator Obama." *Esquire*, June 2008, 109, 114.

Pindell, James. "The Obama Factor." *Campaigns & Elections*, December 2006, 98.

Pitney, John J., Jr. "George W. Obama." *National Review Online*, February 28, 2007, http://www.nationalreview.com (accessed February 28, 2007).

Pleming, Sue. "Rice Hails Obama Race Speech as 'Important' for U.S." *Reuters*, March 28, 2008, http://news.yahoo.com (accessed March 28, 2008).

Powell, Michael. "Following Months of Criticism, Obama Quits His Church." *New York Times*, June 1, 2008, http://www.nytimes.com (accessed June 1, 2008).

Powell, Michael and Jeff Zeleny. "Lesson of Defeat: Obama Comes out Punching." *New York Times*, March 6, 2008, A1.

"Primary Colour." *The Economist*, March 15, 2008, 38.

"Profile: Barack Obama." *BBC News*, January 12, 2007, http://news.bbc.co.uk (accessed January 12, 2007).

"Q & A with Senator Barack Obama." *Chicago Tribune*, June 30, 2005, General Reference Center Gold. Gale (accessed May 20, 2008).

Quindlen, Anna. "A Leap Into the Possible." *Newsweek*, August 9, 2004, 60.

Remnick, David. "Testing the Waters." *New Yorker*, November 6, 2006, http://www.newyorker.com (accessed May 30, 2008).

"Republicans for Obama." *The Nation*, February 25, 2008, http://www.thenation.com (accessed February 26, 2008).

"Rice: Obama Candidacy Signals Progress." *Associated Press*, February 25, 2007. http://www.msnbc.msn.com (accessed February 26, 2007).

Rich, Frank. "Stop Him Before He Gets More Experience." *New York Times*, February 11, 2007, 4.12.

Ripley, Amanda, David Thigpen, and Jeannie McCabe, "Obama's Ascent." *Time*, November 15, 2004, 74–81.

Ripley, Amanda. "A Mother's Story." *Time*, April 21, 2008, 36, 39, 42.

Roach, Ronald. "Obama Rising." *Black Issues in Higher Education*, 2004, 20–23.

Robinson, Eugene. "The Moment for this Messenger?" *Washington Post*, March 13, 2007. A.17.

Rogak, Lisa, ed. *Barack Obama, In His Own Words*. New York: Carroll & Graf, 2007.

Rohter, Larry. "Obama Says Real-Life Experience Trumps Rivals' Foreign Policy Credits." *New York Times*, April 10, 2008, http://www.nytimes.com (accessed April 10, 2008).

Royce, Marc. "Oprah Talks to Barack Obama." *O, the Oprah Magazine*, November 2004, 248.

Rudin, Ken. "Obama or a History of Black Presidents of the U.S." *National Public Radio*, December 7, 2006, http://www.npr.com (accessed December 7, 2006).

Rutenberg, Jim. "Edwards Finally Chooses a Favorite." *New York Times*, May 15, 2008, A.1.

Rutenberg, Jim, and Jeff Zeleny. "The Politics of the Lapel, When it Comes to Obama." *New York Times*, May 15, 2008, A.27.

Scharnberg, Kirsten, and Kim Barker. "The Not-So-Simple Story of Barack Obama's Youth." *Chicago Tribune*, March 25, 2007, http://www.chicagotribune.com (accessed March 25, 2007).

Scheiber, Noam. "Race Against History." *New Republic*, 230, 2004, 21–26.

Scott, Janney. "In Illinois, Obama Proved Pragmatic and Shrewd." *New York Times*, July 30, 2007, http://www.nytimes.com (accessed July 30, 2007).

———. "In 2000, a Streetwise Veteran Schooled a Bold Young Obama." *New York Times*, September 9, 2007, 20.

———. "Memories of Obama in New York Differ." *New York Times*, October 29, 2007, http://www.nytimes.com (accessed October 30, 2007).

———. "A Free-Spirited Wanderer Who Set Obama's Path." *New York Times*, March 14, 2008, http://www.nytimes.com (accessed March 14, 2008).

———. "Obama Chooses Reconciliation Over Rancor." *New York Times*, March 19, 2008, A.14.

Seelye, Katharine Q. "The Casey Endorsement." *New York Times*, March 28, 2008, http://www.nytimes.com (accessed March 28, 2008).

Silverstein, Ken. "Barack Obama Inc." *Harper's Magazine*, November 2006, 31–40.

Sirota, David. "Mr. Obama Goes to Washington." *The Nation*, June 26, 2006, http://www.thenation.com (accessed May 19, 2008).

Slevin, Peter. "Obama Forged Political Mettle in Illinois Capitol." *Washington Post*, February 9, 2007, A01.

Spencer, Jim. "Obama Needs Inspiration to Get His Optimism Across." *Denver Post*, March 19, 2007, B-05.

Stengel, Richard. "Interview with Barack Obama." *Time*, December 10, 2007, 40.

———. "Democracy Reborn." *Time*, February 11, 2008, 6.

Sullivan, Andrew. "Goodbye to All That." *The Atlantic*, December 2007, 46, 48–49.

Szep, Jason, and Ellen Wulfhorst. "Undecided Voters Give Obama Hope in 2008 Race." *Reuters*, November 21, 2007, http://news.yahoo.com (accessed November 21, 2007).

Thomas, Evan, Holly Bailey, and Richard Wolffe "Only in America." *Newsweek*, May 5, 2008, 28.

"The Triumph of Hope Over Experience." *The Economist*, December 15, 2007, 16–18.

Toomey, Shamus. "A Lot To Do With Race." *Chicago Sun Times*, May 5, 2007, http://www.suntimes.com (accessed May 18, 2007).

Trice, Dawn Turner. "Obama Unfazed by Foes' Doubts on Race Question." *Chicago Tribune*, March 15, 2004. Quoted in John K. Wilson, *Barack Obama, This Improbable Quest* (Boulder, CO: Paradigm Publishers, 2008).

Tumulty, Karen. "The Candor Candidate." *Time*, June 11, 2007, 33–34.

———. "The Real Running Mates." *Time*, September 24, 2007, 35, 36.

———. "Out of Reach?" *Time*, October 8, 2007, 50, 52.

———. "Obama Finds His Moment." *Time*, December 10, 2007, 41, 45.

"Verbatim." *Time*, June 16, 2008, 12.

Victor, Kirk. "In His Own Words: Barack Obama." *National Journal*, March 18, 2006, 22–23.

———. "Reason to Smile." *National Journal*, March 18, 2006, 18–27.

Von Drehle, David. "It's Their Turn Now." *Time*, February 11, 2008, 36, 48.

Wallace-Wells, Benjamin. "The Great Black Hope." *Washington Monthly*, November 2004, 30–36.

———. "Obama's Narrator." *New York Times Magazine*, April 1, 2007, 30–35.

Walsh, Kenneth T. "Talkin' 'Bout My New Generation." *U.S. News & World Report*, January 8, 2007, 26–28.

———. "One-on-One with Barack Obama." *U.S. News & World Report*, February 25, 2008, 44.

Walters, Ron. "Barack Obama and the Politics of Blackness." *Journal of Black Studies*, July 18, 2007, 13–14, 17. http://www.jbs.sagepubl.com (accessed July 18, 2007).

Wang, Beverly. "Michelle Obama Says Husband Has Moral Compass." *Associated Press*, May 7, 2007.

Weisskopf, Michael. "How He Learned to Win." *Time*, May 19, 2008, 28–30.

"Where's the Beef?" *The Economist*, April 14, 2007, 36.

Whitesides, John. "Obama, Clinton Side with Anti-War Democrats." *Yahoo News*, May 25, 2007, http://news.yahoo.com (accessed May 25, 2007).

Wikisource Contributors. "Barack Obama's Iraq Speech." *Wikisource, The Free Library*, http://en.wikisource.org (accessed May 9, 2008).

Williams, Michael. "CBS4's One-on-One Interview with Barack Obama." *CBS Television Station Inc.*, May 23, 2008, http://cbs4.com (accessed May 26, 2008).

Wilson, John K. *Barack Obama, This Improbable Quest* (Boulder, CO: Paradigm Publishers, 2008).

Wolffe, Richard. "America Can Be a Force (for) Good in the World." *Newsweek*, April 21, 2008, 24.

———. "Obama's Sister Souljah Moment." *Newsweek*, April 29, 2008, http://www.newsweek.com (accessed April 29, 2008).

Wolffe, Richard, and Daren Briscoe. "Across the Divide." *Newsweek*, July 16, 2007, 22–30, 26, 34.

Wolffe, Richard, and Evan Thomas. "Sit Back, Relax, Get Ready to Rumble." *Newsweek*, May 19, 2008, 21.

Wolffe, Richard, Jessica Ramirez, and Jeffrey Bartholet. "When Barry Became Barack." *Newsweek*, March 22, 2008, http://www.newsweek.com (accessed March 24, 2008).

York, Byron. "Obama Madness," *National Review*, November 20, 2006, 17–18.

"Young Voters Favor Obama, Clinton." *CBS News*, June 26, 2007, http://www.cbsnews.com (accessed June 26, 2007).

Younge, Gary. "The Obama Effect." *The Nation*, December 31, 2007, http://www.thenation.com (accessed December 19, 2007).

Youngman, Sam, and Aaron Blake. "Obama's Crime Votes are Fodder for Rivals." *The Hill*, March 13, 2007, http://www.thehill.com (accessed May 12, 2008).

Zeleny, Jeff "The First Time Around: Senator Obama's Freshman Year," *Chicago Tribune*, December 24, 2005, http://www.chicagotribune.com/news/local/chi-051224obama,0,6232648.story (accessed May 20, 2008).

———. "Testing the Water: Obama Tests His Own Limits." *New York Times*, December 24, 2006, 1.1.

———. "As Candidate, Obama Carves Antiwar Stance." *New York Times*, February 26, 2007, http://www.newyorktimes.com (accessed February 26, 2007).

———. "Obama Highlights His War Opposition." *New York Times*, October 2, 2007, http://www.nytimes.com (accessed October 2, 2007).

———. "Obama Wins in Mississippi." *New York Times*, March 12, 2008, http://www.nytimes.com (accessed March 12, 2008).

———. "Assessing Race in America, Obama Calls Pastor Divisive." *New York Times*, March 18, 2008, A.1.

———. "Obama Leaves the Stage to Mix with His Skeptics." *New York Times*, May 2, 2008, A.17.

Zeleny, Jeff, and John M. Broder. "On Eve of Primary, Clinton Ad Invokes bin Laden." *New York Times*, April 22, 2008, A.23.

Zeleny, Jeff, and Katharine Q. Seelye. "West Virginia's Byrd Supports Obama." *New York Times*, May 19, 2008, http://www.nytimes.com (accessed May 19, 2008).

Zorn, Eric. "Obama Critics Build Case on Faulty Premises." *Chicago Tribune*, December 19, 2006. Quoted in John K. Wilson, *Barack Obama, This Improbable Quest* (Boulder, CO: Paradigm Publishers, 2008).

Index

About the Author

JOANN F. PRICE is a writing coach and author of *Martha Stewart: A Biography* (2007) and *Barack Obama: A Biography* (2008).